Stress in College Athletics
Causes, Consequences, Coping

*Pre-publication
REVIEWS,
COMMENTARIES,
EVALUATIONS . . .*

"**E**xcellent! Good flow and very readable, as well as applicable."

John Swofford, MEd
*Commissioner,
The Atlantic Coast Conference*

"**I** found *Stress in College Athletics* to be a very interesting book. It confirmed many of my thoughts about the high pressures experienced by most of us in college athletics. I was particularly interested to read about the stresses experienced by student-athletes and coaches. As an athletic director, I agree with most of the stress points that were cited in the athletic directors' section, but to appreciate the stresses put on student-athletes by the academic requirements was a good reminder for me about our profession."

Bill Byrne, MBA
*Director of Athletics,
University of Nebraska,
Lincoln*

Stress in College Athletics
Causes, Consequences, Coping

THE HAWORTH PRESS
New, Recent, and Forthcoming Titles
of Related Interest

Alcohol/Chemical Dependency and the College Student edited by Timothy M. Rivinus

Parental Concerns in College Student Mental Health edited by Leighton C. Whitaker

Helping Students Adapt to Graduate School: Making the Grade by Earle Silber

Campus Violence: Kinds, Causes, and Cures edited by Leighton C. Whitaker and Jeffrey W. Pollard

College Student Development edited by Leighton C. Whitaker and Richard E. Slimak

College Student Suicide edited by Leighton C. Whitaker and Richard E. Slimak

The Bulimic College Student: Evaluation, Treatment, and Prevention edited by Leighton C. Whitaker and William N. Davis

Stress in College Athletics
Causes, Consequences, Coping

WITHDRAWN

James H. Humphrey, EdD   Deborah A. Yow, PhD, DHum

William W. Bowden, PhD

The Haworth Half-Court Press
An Imprint of The Haworth Press, Inc.
New York • London • Oxford

Published by

The Haworth Half-Court Press, an imprint of The Haworth Press, Inc., 10 Alice Street, Binghamton, NY 13904-1580.

Cover design by Jennifer M. Gaska.

Library of Congress Cataloging-in-Publication Data

Humphrey, James Harry, 1911-
    Stress in college athletics : causes, consequences, coping / James H. Humphrey, Deborah A. Yow, William W. Bowden.
        p.   cm.
    Includes bibliographical references (p.) and index.
    ISBN 0-7890-0934-X (hb : alk. paper)—ISBN 0-7890-0935-8 (pbk. : alk. paper)
    1. College athletes—Psychology. 2. Stress (Psychology) I. Yow, Deborah A. II. Bowden, William W. III. Title.

GV347 .H86 2000

99-056493

CONTENTS

ABOUT THE AUTHORS

James H. Humphrey, EdD, is Professor Emeritus at the University of Maryland in College Park. He is the author or co-author of more than a dozen books about stress, including *Stress in Coaching,* and his articles and research reports have appeared in more than twenty national and international journals and magazines. Considered a pioneer in stress education, Dr. Humphrey is the founder and editor of *Human Stress: Current Selected Research* and editor of the sixteen-book series *Stress in Modern Society.*

Deborah A. Yow, PhD, DHum, is Director of Intercollegiate Athletics at the University of Maryland. She has served as a coach and teacher at the high school and university levels and began her administrative career as Assistant Director of Gator Boosters at the University of Florida. Dr. Yow was formerly the Associate Director at the University of North Carolina at Greensboro and Director of Intercollegiate Athletics at Saint Louis University. In 1994, she became the first female athletic director in the Atlantic Coast Conference when coming to Maryland. The author of numerous books and articles and a nationally respected speaker, Dr. Yow is a member of the National Collegiate Athletic Association (NCAA) Management Council and other well-known athletic and educational agencies and commissions. In addition, she is President Elect of the National Association of Collegiate Directors of Athletics.

William W. Bowden, EdD, PhD, is founder and president of Strategic Management Consultants, a firm that has worked with dozens of colleges, universities, corporations, and the National Collegiate Athletic Association (NCAA) in relation to their athletics interests and management challenges. The author of more than thirty research reports, articles, and books, Dr. Bowden also served as a teacher and administrator at the university level for seventeen years.

Foreword

The public's perception of stress among athletes, coaches, and administrators and its perception of how effectively these individuals cope with stress often differ from the realities of stress in contemporary athletics. Therefore, the management of stress and the factors within the athletics environment that cause significant stress are subjects of considerable importance for student-athletes, their parents, coaches, and athletics administrators. Indeed, they are highly relevant subjects in which also the health sciences, social sciences, and behavioral sciences have an appropriate and increasing research interest.

In this book, three leading authorities on human stress, intercollegiate athletics, and organizational behavior combine their expertise to address the causes and consequences of stress in collegiate athletics. They also address the coping mechanisms that are effective for stress management in the athletics environment.

One of the primary research methods employed in this book's foundational study was the solicitation of direct and extensive input from athletes, coaches, and athletic administrators. That method gives the book a compelling validity and relevance for those directly involved in athletics, as well as for those who study the field of intercollegiate athletics.

While the comprehensive and detailed contents qualify this book as a scholarly work, it provides practical and useful information in understandable language. The study begins with a definition of stress and the numerous terms that are used to describe stress, followed by an extensive discussion of the perceptions of stress in college athletics. The discussion also focuses on the causes, consequences, and coping mechanisms associated with stress in this environment. This leads to a thorough explanation of the most effective stress-reduction techniques practiced in athletics and elsewhere.

Clearly, the scope and impact of stress in intercollegiate athletics are pervasive problems. This study will be an important step in the ongoing effort to understand and deal with the phenomenon of stress in the athletics experience. The research results and the practical and wise application of those findings to today's athletics environment make this volume highly useful for those who work and participate in the field of athletics. It will also serve as the basis for further research and inquiry in the field of intercollegiate athletics and human stress. It will be a work of lasting value and of broad and significant interest.

Terry Holland
Director of Athletics
University of Virginia

Preface

From its beginnings, college athletics has been a highly stressful environment. Not long after its inception, intercollegiate athletics began to experience complex and troubling issues. In fact, in the early 1900s an athletics scandal related to widespread and serious physical injuries in collegiate athletes during Theodore Roosevelt's administration prompted the President himself to call for greater restraint and control in the conduct of intercollegiate athletics competition. The scope and nature of the challenging issues associated with conducting a major athletics enterprise within an academic setting have continued over the decades since that time—and indeed have broadened and intensified.

Modern-day examples of violations such as point shaving to "throw" games, illegal under-the-table payments to athletes, gambling by student-athletes, circumvention of eligibility standards, violent, abusive and antisocial behaviors, inordinate pressure to win at all costs, and use of alcohol and drugs by some athletes all combine to create significant issues and stress-inducing conditions within college athletics. Studies have indicated that these behaviors are, in part, linked to the aggressive nature of numerous intercollegiate sports and also to the profound stress under which student-athletes often find themselves in highly competitive athletics environments. In addition, the academic challenges that face the student-athlete are a topic of wide discussion and concern.

There is little doubt that stress in modern times is affecting an astounding number of people and that it is the cause of many of the nation's most severe health problems. Indeed, stress is the great disease of our culture. With this idea in mind it is the intent of the authors to explore the phenomenon of stress as it pertains to college athletics.

In order to formulate a useful database for the book the authors surveyed several hundred college athletes, coaches, and athletic directors. We were able to obtain extensive firsthand information with regard to the nature and extent of stress in the college athletics environment. This information included *causes* of stress among those associated with college athletics, its *effects* upon them, and how they attempt to *cope* with it.

Chapter 1 considers important general aspects of stress, including theories of stress and its causes and effects.

Perceptions of stress among coaches, athletic directors, and athletes are discussed in Chapter 2.

Chapters 3 and 4 take into account the causes and consequences of stress among athletes, coaches, and athletic directors as well as how they attempt to cope with stress.

Emotions in college athletics is the subject of Chapter 5. This chapter includes and focuses upon emotional stability and emotional reactivity of coaches during competition.

Chapter 6 considers the subject of a healthful stress-management lifestyle for those involved in college athletics, with discussions about nutrition, diet, body restoration, and physical activity and exercise.

Inducing the relaxation response through the proven techniques of relaxation, meditation, and biofeedback is discussed in Chapters 7, 8, and 9.

The final chapter addresses self-modification of behavior as a stress-reducing technique that can prove to be effective in the athletics environment.

Many of the principles discussed in this volume, especially the stress-management techniques, also have applicability beyond athletics to participants in other fields as well as members of the general public.

Acknowledgments

A book is seldom the sole product of the authors. Granted, the authors do most of the things concerned with actually putting a book together, from the germ of the idea to seeing it through final publication. It is almost always true, however, that many individuals participate, at least indirectly in some way, before a book is finally completed. This volume is no exception. We want to express our sincere appreciation to the hundreds of college athletes, coaches, and athletic directors who willingly gave of their time to participate in our extensive surveys. These sources have been extremely valuable in providing relevant and compelling data for the book. We also acknowledge the beneficial input from Terry Holland and the expert word processing assistance provided by Vernon Krueger in the preparation of this manuscript.

Chapter 1

Understanding Stress

The subject of stress is complicated and complex. It is also a misunderstood subject of considerable interest and extensive discussion in modern society. Therefore, one of the first steps in dealing with the serious human phenomenon of stress is to develop an understanding of it. Essential questions are: What is stress? How do we react to it? What are its causes and effects? What are the effective coping strategies? Each of these questions must be carefully considered.

It is interesting to note that most of the persons in our surveys of stress in college athletics revealed a lack of knowledge about the subject. But they also indicated that they would be interested in understanding the scientific dimensions of stress as well as how they thought they were influenced by stress personally. Individuals involved in college athletics need to understand certain basic and essential factors if they are to deal with stress effectively. Therefore, it seems appropriate to provide some information about the human stress phenomenon. This chapter is devoted to that subject.

THE MEANING OF STRESS AND RELATED TERMS

There has been much confusion surrounding the term *stress* as well as other terms used in connection with it. In fact, Paul J. Rosch, President of the American Institute of Stress, once commented, "Everyone talks about stress, and presumably everyone knows what it is, but in point of fact, no one *knows* what stress is. It not only means different things to different people, it *is* different things to different people."[1] The purpose here is to attempt to clarify some of

1

the existing confusion about the meaning of stress and related terms.

It should be understood at the outset that we are not attempting to develop a set of standardized stress-related terms. This would be almost impossible and, at the same time, probably impractical. As far as this book is concerned, our purpose is chiefly for clarity of communication.

The following discussion of terminology focuses on terms as definitions used by authorities in the fields of stress science and stress management. An attempt will be made in some cases to begin with the rather general meaning and then give it specificity for the subject being addressed.

Stress

There is no universal agreement regarding the derivation of the term stress. Some sources suggest that the term is derived from the Latin word *stringere,* meaning to bind tightly. Other sources contend that the term derives from the French word *destresse,* anglicized to *distress,* and suggest that the prefix *dis* was eventually eliminated.

A common and generalized literal description of stress is "a constraining force or influence." When applied to the human organism, this could be interpreted to mean the extent to which the body can withstand a given force or influence. In this regard, the late Hans Selye, who was generally known as the "Father of Stress," described it as the "nonspecific response of the body to any demand made upon it."[2] This means that stress involves the mobilization of the body's resources in response to some stimulus (stressor). These responses can include various physical and chemical changes. This description of stress could be logically extended by saying that it involves demands that tax or exceed the resources of the human body. (Selye's concept of stress will be explained in more detail later in this chapter.) This means that stress involves these bodily responses, but that it also involves long-term wear and tear on the person brought about by these responses.

In essence, stress can be considered as any factor, acting internally or externally, which makes adaptation to environment difficult and which induces increased effort on the part of the individual to maintain a state of equilibrium between himself or herself and the external environment. It should be understood that stress is a *state* that one is in, and this should not be confused with any agent that produces such a state.[3] Such agents are referred to as stressors.

Understanding the meaning of stress can be made more difficult because certain stress-related terms can cause confusion. Therefore, it seems appropriate at this point to review the meaning of such terms as *tension, emotion, anxiety, depression,* and *burnout.*

Tension

Tension is frequently used in a variety of ways in regard to stress. Tensions can be considered as unnecessary or exaggerated muscle contractions that could be accompanied by abnormally elevated or reduced activities of the internal organs. This means that tension can be viewed in two frames of reference: first, as *physiologic* or *unlearned tensions* and second, as *psychologic* or *learned tensions.* An example of the first, physiologic or unlearned tensions, would be "tensing" at bright lights or intense sounds. Psychologic or learned tensions can be considered as responses to stimuli that ordinarily do not involve muscle contractions, but that sometime earlier in a person's experience were associated with a situation in which tension was a part of the normal response. An example of such tension is an inability to relax when riding in a car after experiencing, witnessing, or imagining a serious automobile accident. Because the brain connects any events that stimulate it simultaneously, this means that, depending upon the unlimited kinds of personal experiences one might have, he or she may show tension to virtually all kinds of stimuli.

In a sense, it may be inferred that physiologic or unlearned tensions are current and spontaneous, while psychologic or learned tensions may be latent as a result of a previous experience and may emerge at a later time. Although to some there may be a slight distinction, perhaps an essential difference between stress and tension is that the former is a physical and/or mental state concerned with wear and tear on the body, while the latter is either a spontaneous or latent condition that can bring about this wear and tear.

Emotion

Since the terms *stress* and *emotion* are used interchangeably in some literature, consideration should be given to the meaning of emotion. Emotion can be viewed as the response an individual makes when confronted with a situation for which he or she is unprepared or which he or she interprets as a possible source of gain or loss. For example, if one is confronted with a situation for which he or she may not have a satisfactory response, the emotional pattern of fear could result. Or, if a person is in a position where desires are frustrated, the emotional phenomenon of anger may occur. Emotion, then, is not the state of stress itself, but rather a stressor that can stimulate stress. (The subject of emotion will be discussed in detail in Chapter 5.)

Anxiety

Another term often used when discussing stress is *anxiety.* In fact, some literature uses the expression "anxiety or stress" implying that they are the same. This can lead to an issue of cause and effect (a version of the chicken and egg controversy). That is, is stress the cause of anxiety or is anxiety the cause of stress?

A basic literal meaning of anxiety is "uneasiness of the mind," but this generalization may be more complex than one might think. C. Eugene Walker, a noted clinical psychologist, points out that psychologists who deal with this subject have difficulty defining the term. His own description of anxiety is "the reaction to a situation where we believe our well-being is endangered or threatened in some way."[4] In *The Language of Feeling,* David Viscott[5] considers anxiety the fear of hurt or loss. He contends that this leads to anger with anger leading to guilt, which if unrelieved, may lead to depression.

Depression

Depression, as used here, is thought of as a painful emotional reaction characterized by intense feelings of loss, sadness, worthlessness, failure, or rejection not warranted by an objective view of events. "Depression is often a disproportionately intense reaction to a difficult life situation. It may be accompanied by such physiological symptoms as tension, slowing of motor and mental activity, fatigue, lack of appetite, and insomnia,"[6] some of the same symptoms accompanying undesirable stress.

Burnout

Some persons become unable to cope with the physical and emotional trauma generated by the demands on their energy, emotions, and time. Current research conducted on people-oriented occupations indicates that some are characterized by several built-in sources of frustration, that eventually lead dedicated workers to become ineffective and apathetic—that is, burned out. Persons who experience *burnout* may begin to perceive their job as impossible. They may begin to question their ability. Feeling helpless and out of control, persons nearing burnout may tire easily and may experience headaches and/or digestive problems.[7] In some cases they will view their tasks and their profession to be increasingly meaningless, trivial, or irrelevant.

With regard to burnout, a recent study of college athletes by William C. Thomas and colleagues is of interest.[8] They hypothesized that the personality trait known as hardiness could mediate the effects of stress that lead to burnout. And further, that hardiness is one characteristic that could differentiate between individuals who are able to effectively manage environmental and internal demands and those who burn out.

The purpose of that study was to examine a theoretical model in which hardiness was posited to act as a stress buffer in the stress-burnout relationship. Participants were 181 NCAA Division I athletes who completed questionnaires containing stress, hardiness, and burnout instruments.

The study revealed that hardiness did appear to act as a buffer against the effect of stress. Given the positive consequences of having a hardier personality, it was concluded that athletes could benefit from purposefully structured experiences to enhance hardiness and improve their ability to cope with the many situational demands placed on them.

Although this brief discussion of certain terms does not exhaust the vocabulary used in relation to stress, it is hoped that it will serve in part to help the reader distinguish the use of terms basic to an understanding of the general subject of stress. Other terminology will be discussed as needed when dealing with certain specific topics of subsequent discussions in this book.

THEORIES OF STRESS

Although it is not our intent to develop a highly technical discourse on the complex and complicated aspects of stress, certain basic understandings need to be taken into account. This requires the use of certain technical terms. For this reason it is appropriate to provide a helpful glossary of terms used in the discussions of the theories of stress that follow these definitions:

> **ACTH** (AdrenoCortico Tropic Hormone)—secreted by the pituitary gland. It influences the function of the adrenals and other glands in the body.
>
> **adrenaline**—A hormone secreted by the medulla of the adrenal glands.
>
> **adrenals**—Two glands in the upper posterior part of the abdomen that produce and secrete hormones. They have two parts, the outer layer—the *cortex,* and the inner core—the *medulla.*
>
> **corticoids**—Hormones produced by the adrenal cortex, an example of which is *cortisone.*
>
> **endocrine**—Glands that secrete their hormones into the bloodstream.
>
> **hormone**—A chemical produced by a gland, secreted into the bloodstream, which influences the function of cells or organs.
>
> **hypothalamus**—The primary activator of the autonomic nervous system, it plays a central role in translating neurological stimuli into endocrine processes during stress reactions.
>
> **pituitary**—An endocrine gland about the size of a pea is located at the base of the brain. It secretes important hormones, one of which is ACTH.

thymus—A ductless gland that is considered a part of the endocrine gland system, located behind the upper part of the breastbone.

There are a variety of theories of stress. One of the better-known, and one to which others are anchored, is the theory of Hans Selye. As mentioned, Selye's description of stress is the "nonspecific response of the body to any demand made upon it." The physiological processes and the reactions involved in Selye's stress model are known as the *General Adaptation Syndrome.* The syndrome has three stages: *alarm reaction, resistance stage,* and *exhaustion.* The relevance of this process to the athletics environment will be discussed in more depth later.

In alarm reaction, the body reacts to the stressor and causes the hypothalamus to produce a biochemical "messenger," which in turn causes the pituitary gland to secrete ACTH into the blood. This hormone then causes the adrenal gland to discharge adrenaline and other corticoids, which causes shrinkage of the thymus with an influence on heart rate, blood pressure, and other physiological responses. It is during this alarm state that functions of the body's immune system can be reduced. Researchers Redford B. Williams and Virginia Williams indicate that this stage and profound stress in general can also trigger abnormal heart rhythms.[9]

Resistance develops if the stressor is not too pronounced. Body adaptation develops to fight back the stress or possibly avoid it, and the body begins to repair any damage.

Exhaustion occurs if there is a prolonged exposure to the same stressor. The ability of adaptation is eventually exhausted and the signs of the first stage (alarm reaction) reappear. Selye contended that our adaptation resources are limited and, when they become irreversible, the result is death.

Selye's stress model, which places emphasis upon "nonspecific" responses, has been widely accepted. However, the nonspecific nature of stress has been questioned by some. This means that psychological stressors activate other endocrine systems in addition to those activated by physiological stressors such as cold, electric shock, and the like.

As in the case of all research, the search for truth will continue. Increasingly precise and sophisticated procedures will emerge in the scientific study of stress. Current theories will be more critically appraised and evaluated and other theories will continue to be advanced. In the meantime, abundant evidence supports the view that uncontrolled stress in modern society is a very serious threat to individual well-being, and of course the individual is the most important factor in such control.

REACTIONS TO STRESS

Reactions to stress can be classified in various ways. As in any kind of classification, some degree of overlapping is unavoidable. For our purposes, we arbitrarily suggest two broad classifications as *physiological* and *behavioral*. Both are applicable to athletics.

Physiological Reactions

Although individuals do not react to stress in the same way physiologically, the following list suggests some of the standard body reactions:

1. Rapid beating of the heart, which has sometimes been described as "pounding of the heart." Athletes and coaches experience this reaction at one time or another as a result of game-related excitement and anticipation.
2. Perspiration, often in the palms of the hands, although profuse sweating may occur in some individuals at other locations on the body. Coaches are sometimes said to "sweat it out" during the most stressful moments of the game.
3. The blood pressure rises, which may be referred to as a hidden reaction because the individual is frequently not aware of this reaction.
4. The pupils of the eyes may dilate. Again, the individual will not necessarily be aware of this.
5. The stomach seems to "knot up," and we tend to refer to this as "feeling a knot in the pit of the stomach." This often has a negative influence on the digestive system.

6. Sometimes individuals experience difficulty in swallowing, which is often characterized as a "lump in the throat."
7. There may be a "tight" feeling in the chest, with accompanying apprehension regarding the seriousness of this reaction.

These various reactions mean that the body is gearing up for a response to a stressor. This phenomenon is called the *fight or flight* response. It was first described a number of years ago as an emergency reaction by Walter B. Cannon,[10] the renowned Harvard University Professor of Physiology. The fight or flight response prepares us for action in the same way that it did for prehistoric man when he was confronted with an enemy. His responses were decided on the basis of the particular situation, such as fighting an opponent for food or fleeing from an animal that provided him with an overmatched and threatening situation. In modern times persons use these same physiological responses to face up to similarly perceived situations. Today we generally do not need to fight physically (although we might feel like it sometimes), or run from wild animals. But our bodies still react with the same fight or flight response. Physiologists point out that we still need this means of self-preservation occasionally, but not as frequently in response to the emotional traumas and anxieties of modern living. However, the acute physical combat that is inherent in some of the contact sports (and often in sports that were originally designed to be limited physical contact sports) presents athletes with challenges that engender responses similar to the basic instincts and reactions of the more primitive mode and environment.

Behavioral Reactions

In discussing behavioral reactions, it should be mentioned again that various degrees of unavoidable overlapping may occur between these reactions and physiological reactions. Although behavioral reactions are, for the most part, physically oriented, they are likely to involve more overt manifestations than are provoked by the physiological reactions. For purposes of this discussion we consider behavior to mean anything that one does as a result of some sort of stimulation.

A person under stress will function with a behavior that is different from ordinary behavior. These behaviors can arbitrarily be subclassified as: counter (sometimes referred to as defensive behavior), dysfunctional, and overt (sometimes referred to as expressive behavior).

In counter behavior, a person will sometimes take action that is intended to counteract the stressful condition. For example, an individual may take a defensive position such as practicing an "on-the-spot" relaxation technique, yet is unaware of it. The person may take a deep breath and silently "count to ten" before taking some action, if any. We sometimes witness this reaction when a coach is displeased with an official's call. (A frequent comment by television analysts when this occurs is: "Coach So and So is livid.") But the coach may often contain himself or herself until an opportune moment arises to protest (often vigorously) the call.

Dysfunctional behavior involves reacting in a manner that demonstrates impaired or abnormal functioning, resulting in a lower level of skill performance than the individual is ordinarily capable of accomplishing. A change in normal speech patterns or a temporary loss of memory may occur. Many of us have experienced this at one time or another due to a profoundly stress-inducing situation—with a "mental block" causing some degree of frustration while we attempt to get back on the original process or sequence of thought. Some football coaches have reported to us that, much to their chagrin, this has happened during games and/or at halftime because of a particularly stressful series of events or a particularly traumatic singular event.

Overt behavior exhibits such reactions as distorted facial expressions (e.g., tics and twitches, profound grimacing, and biting the lip), frequent spitting, shaking of one's fists, or flailing of the arms. There appears to be a need for a person to move about, thus pacing around is characteristic of this condition. Overt behavior in the form of these activities is perceived by some coaches and athletes as highly effective in reducing pressure, threat, and distress.

A point of interest here is that some chair-bashing and foot-stomping coaches may be relieving themselves of stress, although such antics may be unacceptable to some officials and fans, as well as being stress-inducing to their student-athletes.

CLASSIFICATIONS OF STRESS

The difficulty encountered in attempting to devise an infallible classification system for the various kinds of stress lies in the fact that it is practically impossible to fit a given type of stress into one exclusive category, due to the possibilities of overlapping. Any such classification on our part is purely arbitrary. Others may wish to make different classifications than those used here and, in the absence of anything resembling standardization, it is their prerogative to do so. Some general classifications of stress that we will deal with in the following discussion are: (a) desirable and undesirable stress, (b) physical stress, (c) psychological stress, and (d) social stress. It should be understood that this does not exhaust the possibility of various kinds of stress. That is, this particular listing is not necessarily theoretically complete, but will serve well for our purposes.

Desirable and Undesirable Stress

The classic comment by Selye that "stress is the spice of life," sums up the idea that stress can be desirable as well as undesirable, invigorating and motivating as well as debilitating. He went on to say that the only way one could avoid stress would be to never attempt to achieve anything and that certain kinds of activities have a beneficial influence in keeping the stress mechanism viable and in balance.

Certainly, the human body needs to be exercised and even challenged in order to function well, and it is a well-known fact in physiological science that muscles will soon atrophy if not subjected to sufficient use. Athletes and coaches express a desirable aspect of stress when they refer to "getting up" for a game, and feeling the "juices flowing." This can also affect athletics administrators similarly, particularly related to athletics events of considerable scope and importance to them and their athletics program.

At one time or another every coach and athlete has experienced "butterflies in the stomach" when faced with a particularly challenging competitive event. Thus, it is important that we understand that stress is a perfectly normal human state and that the body is under various degrees of stress in those conditions that are potentially related to happiness as well as those related to disappointment and sadness.

To illustrate this point in an athletics environment, the following scenario was devised by the distinguished psychologist, George W. Knox:

> It is the last moment of a championship basketball game; the biochemistry of the two teams is roughly equal. One shot occurs and one team wins by one point. Immediately, one team is in a state of extreme happiness. Healthful endorphins saturate their bloodstreams. The other team immediately goes into intense depression and their bloodstreams become saturated with depression-associated harmful substances.[11]

In the literature, undesirable stress may be referred to as distress. Selye, for example, referred to the pleasant or healthy kind of stress as *eustress*, and to the unpleasant or unhealthy kind as *distress*.

We have mentioned some of the desirable features of stress, but as any influence involving the human organism, almost anything in sustained excess is harmful and counterproductive. This certainly is true in the case of abnormal amounts of stress. When stress becomes prolonged and unrelenting, and thus chronic, it can result in very serious health issues for the individual.

It has been suggested that what we ordinarily refer to as aging may be nothing more than the sum total of all the scars left by the stress of life. This could be why some relatively young athletics coaches who have been subjected to prolonged and intensive stress may "look old for their years." In the final analysis, the recommendation is not necessarily to avoid stress, but to prevent it from becoming a chronic condition—with all of the physiological and psychological impact that such stress can produce.

Although both "good" stress and "bad" stress place specific demands for resources on the body, does it mean that good stress is "safe" and bad stress "dangerous"? In 1981, two prominent psychologists explored this question. Israel Posner and Lewis A. Leitner[12] made some interesting suggestions in this regard. They believed that two psychological variables, *predictability* and *controllability*, play an important role.

It can be reasoned that predictable pain and discomfort are less stressful because under this condition a person is said to be capable of learning when it is safe to relax and "lower his or her guard." Since periods of impending pain are signaled, the person can safely relax at times when the warning signal is absent. These periods of psychological safety seem to insulate individuals from harmful effects of stress. Obviously, persons receiving unsignaled pain have no way of knowing when it is safe to relax and thus are more likely to develop serious health problems as a result of the chronic psychological stress. In almost all cases, a coach or athlete should be able to predict when he or she is going into a crucial athletics contest or other related stressful situation. This predictability, though relative, should be somewhat enabling with regard to their profoundly stressful experiences.

The second psychological variable, controllability of environmental stressors (which is closely related to coping behavior) also plays a major role in determining the level of stress effects. The ability to control painful events may to some degree insulate individuals from experiencing the damaging effects of stress. However, such coping behavior is beneficial only if a person is given a feedback signal that informs him or her that the coping response was successful in avoiding an impending stressor. Without this heartening feedback, any active coping behavior may increase stress effects, since it profoundly calls upon the energy reserves of the body (and emotions) and might leave the individual in a state of chronic stress.

The research on predictability and controllability of stressful events may help answer why people who purposely seek out stressful and challenging activities do not appear to develop stress-related illnesses from this form of stress. In contrast, when essentially similar body reactivity is produced by "bad" stress (stress that has neither predictability nor controllability and produces predominantly negative outcomes), then stress-related illnesses will often result. Perhaps "good" stress does not produce illness because typically the events associated with it are planned in advance (they are predictable) or otherwise scheduled or integrated (they are controlled) into the individual's life. However, even activities that are generally considered to be pleasant and exciting (good stress) can produce illness if the individual is not forewarned or has little or no control over the events. Unpleasant events (bad stress) may result in stress-related illness because they generally come without warning and cannot be controlled.

The previous discussion could have been the basis for the following comments made by a well-known football coach: "Coaching does not create stress. If you are organized and have a plan you should not be stressed. My personal opinion is that there are many more stressful occupations than coaching." (Incidentally, this statement was made about three months *after* this coach had been released from his job.)

Finally, we should mention that some persons have taken the middle ground on this subject by saying that stress is neither good nor bad, indicating that the effect of stress is not determined by the stress itself, but by how it is viewed and processed by the individual. That is, we either handle stress effectively or we allow it to influence us negatively, and thus become victims of undesirable stress.

Physical Stress

In discussing physical stress, we should differentiate between the terms *physical* and *physiological*. The former should be considered a broad term and can be described as "pertaining to or relating to the body." On the other hand, the term physiological is concerned with how the organs of the body relate to one another. Therefore, physical stress could be related to unusual and excessive physical exertion, as well as by certain physiological conditions brought about by some kind of stress.

Although there are many kinds of physical stress, they can be divided into two general types: *emergency* stress (short term and often high impact) and *continuing* stress. In emergency stress, the previously described physiological reactions take place. That is, when an emergency arises, such as bodily injury, hormones are discharged into the bloodstream. This involves an increase in heart rate, rise in blood pressure, and dilation of the blood vessels in the muscles to prepare themselves for immediate use of the energy that is generated.

In continuing stress, the body reaction is more complicated. The physiological involvement is the same, but more and more hormones continue to be produced, the purpose of which is to increase body resistance. In cases where the stress is excessive (such as an extensive third-degree burn or an athletics season with prolonged difficulties and undesired outcomes), a third phase in the form of exhaustion of the adrenal glands can develop, sometimes culminating in physical and/or mental deterioration.

We have said that physical stress can be concerned with unusual and excessive exertion. This can be shown in a general way by performing an experiment involving fairly mild physical exertion. First try to find your resting pulse. This can be done by placing your right wrist, palm facing you, in your left hand. Now, bring the index and middle fingers of your left hand around the wrist and press lightly until you feel the beat of your pulse. Next, time this beat for ten seconds and then multiply this figure by six. This will give you your resting pulse rate per minute. For example, if you counted twelve beats in ten seconds, your resting pulse is seventy-two beats per minute. The next step is to engage in some physical activity. Stand and balance yourself on one foot. Hop up and down on this foot for a period of about twenty seconds, or less if it is too strenuous. Then, take your pulse again in the same manner suggested above. You will find that as a result of this activity your pulse rate will be elevated above your resting pulse. Even with this small amount of physical exertion, the body was adjusting to cope with it, as evidenced by the rise in pulse rate. This was noticeable to you. However, other events such as a slight rise in blood pressure were likely involved, and were probably not as noticeable to you.

Psychological Stress

The main difference between physical and psychological stress is that the former involves a real situation, while psychological stress is more concerned with foreseeing or imagining a stressful situation. For example, a vicarious experience of danger may be of sufficient intensity to cause muscle tension and elevate the heart rate.

It has been clearly demonstrated that prolonged and unrelenting nervous tension developing from psychological stress can result in

mental anguish, which in turn can cause various serious heath problems.

It should be mentioned that historically, physiological and psychological conceptions of stress have evolved independently within
their respective fields. However, efforts are being made to integrate
these two conceptions for the purpose of emphasizing the continu-
ity between physiological and psychological theory.

Social Stress

Humans are profoundly social beings. They do things together.
They play together. They work in concert for the benefit of society.
They have fought together in times of national emergency in order
to preserve the kind of society in which they believe. This means
that life involves a constant series of social interactions. These
interactions involve a two-way street, in that the individual has
some sort of impact upon society and in turn society has an influence upon the individual. Obviously many levels of social stress
occur in life situations. For example, shifting social and value para-
digms, economic conditions, and uncertain other social issues have
been found to be stressful challenges for individuals. Specifically,
numerous possibilities exist for social stress in the coaching profession, especially since coaches are expected to interact with myriads
of individuals and groups such as players, parents, boosters, staff
members, the media, the faculty, and alumni, along with a host of
others. This is also true for athletics administrators, especially athletic directors, as well as student-athletes to some degree.

Negative attitudes resulting from failed or ineffective social
interactions will almost always generate disappointment, hard feelings, and hostility among individuals and groups, making for more
stressful conditions for all concerned. Also, a neutral or laissez-faire
attitude often degenerates into indifferent tolerance and, as such,
can become almost as debilitating as a negative attitude. In fact, the
development of an "I don't care" attitude can often make life intol-
erable and bring about stress.

In the final analysis, people themselves hold the key to the avoidance of undesirable social stress in any kind of environment. In the
athletics environment, the challenge is to maintain balance and a
positive attitude in the face of the almost incessant public, media,

social, and relational regimen that is required of coaches and athletic directors—and to some extent also, the high profile student-athlete.

CAUSES OF STRESS

When reviewing the causes of stress, a fair and reasonable question might be: What *doesn't* cause stress? This is mentioned because most human environments as well as society as a whole are now seen as stress-inducing to some degree. In recent years so many causes of cancer have been identified that it seems "almost everything causes cancer." Perhaps the same could be said of stress. Because it seems to have reached "epidemic" proportions, it is easy to believe that "almost everything causes stress."

In the past several years researchers have studied certain life events as causes of stress. Through life-events scales, they have attempted to find out what kinds of health problems are associated with various events, normal and abnormal, that occur to people either in the regular course of life or as a result of mistakes and various kinds of misfortune.

As important as life-events scales are as a means of detecting causes of stress, they are not without their critics. Some feel that rather than life events, a better course is to measure day-to-day problems. These daily problems are sometimes referred to as "daily hassles," the common concerns in everyday living rather than the high impact, stress-inducing life events.

EFFECTS OF STRESS

The viewpoint that prompts the comment: "almost everything causes stress," could be applied with the assertion that "stress causes everything." One tragic consequence is that stress-related psychological and physiological disorders are now viewed as primary social and health problems. Compelling evidence from studies and clinical trials, as well as many standard medical textbooks, attribute anywhere from 50 to 80 percent of all diseases at least in part to stress-related origins.

The literature by various medical authorities shows that among other conditions, the following in some way could be stress related: diabetes, cirrhosis of the liver, high blood pressure, peptic ulcer, migraine headaches, multiple sclerosis, herpes, lung disease, injury due to accidents, mental health problems, cancer, and coronary heart disease. Specifically, in the case of coronary heart disease it was once reported that included in the statistics of middle-aged male deaths resulting from coronary disease were a number of athletics coaches who suffered heart attacks while involved in athletics events or while fulfilling other coaching responsibilities.[13]

Finally, we have attempted to define stress and to review some of the dynamics and results of stress. As we view stress and its powerful effects on the human body and then integrate the survey results from coaches, student-athletes, and athletic administrators, we will bring into focus the relevance and compelling importance of this subject in the area of college athletics.

Chapter 2

Perceptions of Stress in College Athletics

Since the term stress appears to have different meanings, we considered it appropriate to accrue some idea of the concepts of stress held by coaches, athletic directors, and athletes. This was accomplished by requesting that the respondents to our surveys complete the following sentence: "Stress is _____."

As expected, a wide variety of responses occurred among and within these three groups, representing their concept of stress.

Our conclusions regarding how coaches, athletic directors, and athletes perceived stress focused on the number of times certain key words emerged in their responses. By identifying such key words it was believed that we could obtain a reasonably valid assessment of each group's conception of stress. (Note: In all instances where respondents could make more than one choice, the total percentages exceed 100 percent. This applies to all responses.)

PERCEPTIONS OF COACHES

Pressure

The word *pressure* appeared in almost one-half of the responses from coaches. This was by far the most frequently used key word and by a margin of about 12 percent more than the second and third key words combined. This is interesting because the word pressure rarely appears in the literature on stress except when it is used in connection with blood pressure. It is also interesting to note that one of the definitions of the term in most standard dictionaries considers it in relation to the human body by referring to pressure as "burden of physical and mental distress."

Coaches are certainly familiar with the word pressure. For example, we frequently see that a certain coach "resigned under pressure." Also they speak of pressure defenses and the full-court press(ure). And, of course, they are constantly under pressure to win. Pressure referred to the *sources* or *kinds* of pressure upon them and also was referred to as the varying stages of *internal* pressure of a mental nature (sometimes with troubling physical symptoms) that they sensed—from fairly mild to acute. Some representative examples of how coaches used the word pressure in describing their concept of stress follow.

Stress is:

- The pressure placed on you to win
- Pressure brought about by the importance put on your work by other people
- A kind of pressure that we feel at times
- Pressure put on oneself by self-determination or by others; it affects your health and happiness and will kill you if you can't offset it
- Pressure put on a person by himself and those around him
- Pressure felt to succeed
- A feeling of tightening pressure in my stomach or head whether internally or externally
- Pressure you feel is mostly self-imposed
- Pressure of having to get something accomplished without proper tools
- The pressure put on a person by both personal goals and outside situations that affect the achieving of the aims of oneself
- The mental and physical pressures involved in performing one's job
- The palpable pressure one feels on a day-to-day basis
- Internal emotional pressure that can cause one to be less productive and produce both physical and mental fatigue

Tension

The key word appearing second most frequently at an 18 percent rate was tension. (This term was described in Chapter 1, p. 3.) Most often the coaches who used the word tension did so in the following manner.

Stress is:

- Tension that brings on a burden of distress
- The inability to handle the tension that a coach has to deal with on a day-to-day basis
- Tension that can lead to distortion of reasoned and rational response to external events
- Meeting situations where tension is developed
- Tension put on yourself by others or self
- A buildup of tension

Anxiety

Closely following tension as a key descriptor was the word anxiety, used at a rate of 17 percent. (This term was described in Chapter 1, p. 4.)

Anxiety can occur when a person is faced with more stress than he or she can handle. Although a certain amount of anxiety is normal and probably unavoidable, it can become a stress-related and serious problem when it is inappropriate or out of proportion to a situation or when it interferes with normal activities. Excessive anxiety may be occurring when the following symptoms are noticed:

- Irritability and tension
- Insomnia
- Excessively demanding attitude
- Loss of appetite
- Restlessness
- Headaches
- Unwarranted concern about physical ailment

It is important to remember that these are also symptomatic of a variety of other types of disorders. The following are some representative examples of how coaches used the word anxiety in their concept of stress.

Stress is:

- Mental anxiety
- Anxiety that affects you physically or mentally
- A cause of anxiety
- One of the outcomes of anxiety that seems to be a part of this business
- Anxiety brought on by situations in which control is not possible
- Anxiety that can cause a coach not to be successful

Conflict and Frustration

Next on the list of key words, each at 8 percent of the time, were conflict and frustration. When stress is induced as a result of the individual not being able to meet needs (basic demands) and satisfy desires (wants and wishes), frustration or conflict results. Frustration occurs when a need is not met and conflict results when choices must be made between nearly equally attractive alternatives or when basic emotional forces oppose one another.

In an emotionally healthy person, the degree of frustration is ordinarily in proportion to the intensity of the need or desire. That is, he or she will objectively observe and evaluate a situation to ascertain whether a solution is possible and, if so, what solution would best enable him or her to achieve fulfillment of needs or desires. Some examples of how coaches used the terms conflict and frustration follow.

Stress is:

- Concerned with conflicts that need to be handled
- Internal conflict caused by many things in my work, and ultimately in my personal life and family
- A condition that can cause conflict

- Frustration after not doing well or not being successful
- Frustration you get from losing
- Frustration caused when you have a serious conflict about your work and its demands

Strain and Worry

Two other key words used, each at 6 percent of the time, were strain and worry. The term strain in the *physical dimension* tends to be used in connection with unusual tension in a muscle caused by overuse or because of a sudden unaccustomed movement. (A strain is a milder injury than a sprain in which ligaments around a joint are pulled or torn, and swelling occurs.) Strain can also refer to some form of perceived mental stress.

Worry can be considered as an imaginary form of fear and it can be a fear not always aroused directly from a person's immediate environment. The following are some examples of how coaches used these words in describing their concept of stress.

Stress is:

- A mental strain
- The strain brought about when one is not successful
- A strain on your health
- A strain on a person because of worry
- A cause for worry when you lose
- A condition with useless worry about winning
- Worrying about your ability to get something done successfully
- The worry and strain that results from the expectations of myself and others related to my job

Key Word Not Used

About 26 percent of the time coaches did not use any of the above key words in indicating what stress means to them. The following are several of these descriptors of stress as they were expressed by coaches.

Stress is:

- Involved with the many problems to be handled in coaching
- Being placed in situations that create hyper conditions

- Trying to accomplish what is expected with personnel not equal to the task
- Inability to have total control of situations
- Manufactured by the pride within each individual coach to be the very best
- Every day of basketball season
- Any event, person, or thing that changes the way things are or how you hope them to be
- Functioning in high gear for a prolonged period of time while attempting to deal with problems and challenges attacking your mental and physical capacities
- Not enough hours in a day
- When responsibility of those you are working with ceases to take place
- Feeling that you cannot control the things that are your responsibility and having inadequate time to perform important tasks
- A pain in the neck
- The result of trying to stuff thirty pounds into a ten-pound bag

In the preceding discussion the perceptions of stress were presented as an aggregate to include all coaches—male and female. At this point it seems appropriate to cite these data for female coaches, as well as to make comparisons with male coaches. The information in Table 2.1 is provided for this purpose.

Table 2.1. Comparison of Perceptions for Female and Male Coaches

Key Word	Percent for Females	Percent for Males
Pressure	40	57
Tension	8	10
Anxiety	7	10
Conflict and Frustration	10	6
Strain and Worry	5.4	6.6
Key Word Not Used	28	26

PERCEPTIONS OF ATHLETIC DIRECTORS

Pressure

The key word pressure occurred in 40 percent of the responses of athletic directors. The following examples indicate ways in which they used the word.

Stress is:

- The pressure I feel from demanding coaches and unhappy student-athletes
- An accumulation of pressure from deadlines, expectations, and challenges of many kinds continuously
- Pressure you allow to bother you
- Pressure that builds up whenever you cannot effectively control situations
- The feeling of pressure in dealing with day-to-day operations and budget issues
- Pressure caused by an inability to control activities
- The pressure to achieve increasingly challenging goals under different parameters
- Emotional pressure
- Mental pressure caused by external forces
- Pressure created in one's mind because of job responsibilities
- A physical response to perceived external pressure
- Pressure from alumni, fans, and the media
- Important to relieving the pressure you feel on your job
- A feeling that you must deal with pressure constantly
- Unrelenting pressure that is harmful to you

Tension

The key word tension appeared second most frequently, 17 percent of the time. A number of the athletic directors who used this word did so in the following manner.

Stress is:

- Physical or mental conditions that cause tension on oneself
- Tension that you allow to bother you
- Feeling tension and overwork
- Tension on the job
- An experience that causes physical tension
- The tension created by having limited ability to control one's own fate
- Physical or mental tension caused by either outside or self-inflicted circumstances over which an individual has little control
- A lot of tension at one time
- A combination of unfavorable events that cause tension

Emotion

Appearing in about 15 percent of the responses was the word emotion, used as follows.

Stress is:

- An emotional experience related to your job
- Emotional factors that create problems
- Emotions that upset you
- Something that increases emotional tension
- Emotional responses to situations that occur in everyday life and work
- A bad emotional experience
- A condition that causes emotional outbursts

It might be mentioned here that emotion is an experience and a descriptor that permeates the athletics environment in many institutions. This is the case in part because of the following: the intense passion that surrounds and characterizes the strong feelings of fans, boosters, athletes, and coaches during competitive events; the sometimes hostile or otherwise inappropriate posture that the media takes on sports issues (for example, attempting to create or expand upon controversy in a manner which is not supported by the facts); and coaches under pressure or duress. This overexercise of passion/emotion in the collegiate setting, when carried to its extreme, is frequently counterproductive to conducting a balanced and healthy athletics enterprise in the context of an academic institution. This is because inappropriate levels of passion related to recruiting, winning/losing, and other issues and outcomes tend to overshadow concerns for academic issues, behavior and citizenship issues, sportsmanship, student-athlete/coach/administrator welfare, and balance in the image of the institution. Rationality, balance, and reason are needed antidotes for some of the overt and irrational emotion and the undue passion that tends to diminish or even subvert the essential purpose of athletics in a college or university setting. With increasing frequency the question is being asked: What is the role and purpose of an athletics program conducted within the context of a college or university? John Gerdy says that ". . . only one of the justifications for athletics being a part of higher education is being met—the justification of providing entertainment."[1] This would be debated by many and perhaps is not the case in athletics programs where there is appropriate attention to student-athlete welfare—that is, to the academic progress and plenary development of the student-athlete.[2] (Note: The subject of emotion will be dealt with in more detail in Chapter 5.)

Anxiety

Anxiety appeared in about 11 percent of the definitions, with the following as examples.

Stress is:

- Anxiety brought about by failure to meet multiple expectations
- Undisciplined mental anxiety combined with fear
- Any anxiety that causes a person to feel concerned or threatened in decision making
- Mental anxiety that brings on strain
- Demands caused by anxiety

Conflict, Frustration, and Worry

Conflict, frustration, and worry each were reported at about 8 percent of the time. They were used in the following manner.

Stress is:

- Problems created by worrying about the future
- When there is a form of conflict
- Associated with the continuous worry regarding student-athletes' welfare, budgets, etc.
- Frustration caused by a lack of resources and time to do a good job

Key Word Not Used

About 20 percent of the athletic directors used none of the key words. The following are several examples of these stress concepts.

Stress is:

- Letting matters affect you to the point that it could be un-healthy for you
- A part of the athletic director's job almost every day
- An extremely upsetting condition caused by adverse external factors
- Handling very difficult problems
- When problems are on your desk and you can't resolve them within your time frame
- Having to make decisions about other people's careers and their ability to earn income
- Something you experience if you let things get out of control
- Having to work with incompetent individuals who generally possess an egocentric mind
- Attempting to deal with situations beyond your control

PERCEPTIONS OF ATHLETES

Pressure

As with coaches and athletic directors, the key word pressure (used at 25.5 percent) was the most prevalent for athletes. The following are examples of how it was used.

Stress is:

- When you feel pressure from anything
- Having way too much pressure on your mind
- When you are put in any pressure situation, especially to win
- The feeling you get when pressured for performance
- The pressure felt on a person due to the workload with sports, school, and job
- Any pressure you have
- When you are carrying a lot of pressure
- Pressure on you that you have trouble either solving or understanding
- Pressure to do too much and not enough time to do it
- Pressure that is put on you mentally and physically
- Pressure that is created by school, peers, deadlines, and football
- A feeling of pressure caused by environmental factors
- Any action where one places pressure on oneself to complete a task
- The result of internal and external pressure
- The pressure you feel to perform to the best of your ability

Anxiety

The key word anxiety was second among athletes at a 13 percent occurrence rate. It was expressed in the following examples.

Stress is:

- A mechanism for coping with perceived anxiety
- Anything that causes anxiety
- Becoming upset with anxiety
- Anxiety over the feeling of not accomplishing goals
- Something that causes you to feel anxiety

Overwhelm

A key word not used by coaches or athletic directors, but used 16 percent of the time by athletes, was some form of the word overwhelm. (The word whelm, by itself, is defined in dictionaries as "to engulf with disastrous effects.") It carries with it the sense of some level of exasperation or hopelessness—and in interviews with student-athletes was clearly described as a precursor to despondency or depression in the case of some of the individuals. The following are some examples of its use.

Stress is:

- When you are completely overwhelmed and all you can do is get upset
- An overwhelming feeling you get over situations you cannot control
- When you are overwhelmed by tasks and aggravation sets in
- The feeling of being overwhelmed when you have a lot of things to accomplish
- When you feel like everything is overwhelming you and there are not enough hours in the day to accomplish them
- Feeling overwhelmed by what is going on in your life

Frustration

Frustration appeared 10 percent of the time, with the following samples selected from the responses.

Stress is:

- Having a feeling of frustration because of academic and athletics problems
- Being frustrated because you have no time to do what you want to do
- The frustration of having sport stress that piles up with school stress
- An overabundance of thoughts and activities that make you frustrated and angry
- A feeling of frustration caused by having too many things to complete
- When you feel frustrated over things out of your control

Conflict, Worry, and Tension

Conflict, worry, and tension each appeared about 7 percent of the time and were expressed as follows.

Stress is:

- A problem in which things worry you
- Getting overly worried about an upcoming event
- When your mental worries wear down your overall condition
- Anything that makes you worry and gives you a headache
- Physical and mental tension
- Tension caused by school and athletics problems
- Anything that causes tension and mental or physical discomfort
- Conflict over what you go through when you have a lot of things to do
- Caused by a conflict when you have too many things on your mind
- A conflict that adds difficulty to your life

Key Word Not Used

About one-fourth of the athletes used no particular key word in expressing their concept of stress. Some of these responses were as follows.

Stress is:

- When the mind realizes that you have so much to do and the body realizes it is physically impossible
- Having way too much on your mind and weighing down on your body
- Being involved in too many activities and getting freaked out about it
- A feeling caused by certain stimuli
- When you get that weird feeling in your stomach
- Anything that hinders your performance in class and on the field
- A barrier that complicates life and causes setbacks

In the preceding discussion about how athletes perceive stress, their perceptions were given as an aggregate to indicate all athletes—male and female. Table 2.2 shows a comparison of responses by gender.

Table 2.2. Comparison of Perceptions for Female and Male Athletes

Key Word	Percent of Females	Percent of Males
Pressure	23	28
Anxiety	12	13
Overwhelm	28	4
Frustration	9	12
Conflict	9	7
Worry	7	6
Tension	7	7
Key Word Not Used	35	24

SUMMARY

In summarizing the responses of all groups (coaches, athletic directors, and athletes), two rather interesting items of information emerged. First, there were relatively few who perceived any aspect of stress as positive. That is, the responses predominantly perceived stress as always being undesirable, with little or no positive effects. (Recall that in Chapter 1, p. 12, we discussed eustress and distress, considered to be good and bad forms of stress.)

Second, in a large percentage of the cases, concepts of stress tended to focus on the stressor rather than on the condition of stress itself. This would appear to be natural because only in relatively recent years has there been adequate research and literature on the subject of stress and how it affects the human body.[3] Nevertheless, the responses of coaches, athletic directors, and athletes about their concepts of stress provided the authors with replete and important guidelines in preparing the content for this book. Because of this, the collection of such data was clearly a worthwhile undertaking. In fact, respondents said that completing this item on the survey as well as other items on the inquiry form caused them to think more meaningfully about stress, and in some cases, to focus on the issue for the first time and address or resolve their feelings about the stress under which they functioned.

Chapter 3

Stress Among College Athletes

In this chapter we will examine those aspects of stress that are of major concern to college athletes—causes, consequences, and coping. The study included the stress phenomenon in both male and female athletes. It is therefore important at the outset to discuss some gender differences, including those differences with reference to stress.

GENDER DIFFERENCES

There are of course structural (anatomical) and functional (physiological) gender differences. However, because these differences are well-known, we will make reference to them only in regard to differences first in several of the basic physical skill performances between males and females.

In the basic locomotor skill of running little difference occurs in performance of boys and girls of elementary school age. However, after that time boys increase their speed and endurance at a rate greater than the increase among girls. Although this may be true on the average, it must be recognized that many girls become excellent performers in distance running. For example, three decades ago it would have been outside the realm of general acceptance that women would be capable of effectively running a marathon. Recently, world-class female marathoners regularly are timed in what would have been credible performance for males in the past.

In the skill of jumping there are many levels in performance of children. Generally speaking, they tend to improve their performance as they get older. This improvement tends to be more pronounced for boys.

In the propulsion skills, especially throwing, gender differences in the performance level among children substantially favors boys. At all age levels, boys are generally better at throwing for distance than girls, but there is not such a pronounced gender difference in throwing for accuracy.

In order to have a more complete understanding of the whole area of gender differences we need to start at birth. From a growth and development viewpoint, at birth the female is from one-half to one centimeter less in length than the male and weighs about 300 grams less, but she is actually a better-developed organism. Thus, on the average, at the time of entrance into school, the female is usually six to twelve months more physically mature than the male. As a result, girls tend to learn earlier how to perform such tasks of manual dexterity as buttoning their clothing. In one of the authors' own observational studies of preschool children some years ago, it was found that girls were able to perform the task of tying their shoelaces at a rate of almost four times that of boys.

Due to selected hormonal influences, boys tend to be more aggressive, restless, and impatient. In addition, the male has more rugged bone and muscle structure, and as a consequence has greater strength than a female of equal age and health. Because of this, males tend to display greater muscular reactivity that in turn expresses itself in a greater tendency toward restlessness and vigorous activity. This capacity among young males is also related to the greater oxygen consumption required to fulfill the male's apparent need for increased energy production. The male body might be compared to an engine that operates at higher levels of torque and speed than the female body. In 1968, the late Franklin Henry of the University of California indicated that males have what might be termed an "active response set," whereas females might have a "reactive response set." This could be interpreted to mean that males confront the environment with an activity orientation while females have a response orientation. Later research indicates that this trait can be linked to societal influences related to perceived, acceptable roles for males and females.

Another factor to take into account is the difference in basal metabolic rate (BMR). The BMR is indicative of the speed at which body fuel is changed into energy, as well as the speed at which this energy is used. BMR can be measured in terms of calories per meter of body surface with a calorie representing a unit measure of heat energy in food. It has been found that on average, from birth to about three years of age BMR rises and then starts to decline until the ages of approximately twenty to twenty-four. The BMR is higher for boys than for girls. Because of the higher BMR, boys will in turn have a higher amount of raw physical energy to expend. Because of differences in sex hormonal conditions and BMR, it appears logical to assume that these factors will influence the male in his behavior and physical performance patterns. Add to these factors the societal influences and we begin to understand these gender differences.

Some studies have shown that as far as hyperactivity is concerned, boys are more hyperactive than girls by a ratio of as much as 9 to 1. This may be the reason why teachers generally tend to rate young males as being so much more aggressive than females, with the result that young boys are observed displaying a higher level of extroverted, aggressive, and sometimes socially negative behaviors. Because of these characteristics, boys generally have poorer relationships with their teachers than do girls, and have behavior problems and resulting disciplinary actions imposed. In the age range from five to nine, boys account for twice as many disturbances as girls in structured settings such as the classroom. This factor is highly significant because good teacher-pupil relationships tend to raise the achievement levels. This is the case for both sexes.

Various studies have shown that girls in K through 8 generally receive higher grades than boys, despite the fact that boys may have intelligence to achieve as well.[1] It is also clearly evident that boys in the early years fail twice as often as girls even when there are no significant differences between intelligence and general achievement test scores of both sexes. This suggests that even though both sexes may have the same intellectual tools, other factors perhaps militate against learning as far as boys are concerned.

Although all of this may be true for preteen boys, the situation seems to change for girls after about thirteen years of age. After that time many aspects of society become anxiety provoking and role modifying for girls. This may be especially true of the school environment. Research in recent years on this subject has revealed some interesting results, some of which can be summarized as follows:

1. There is insufficient encouragement for girls to pursue mathematics and science.
2. There are subtle teacher practices, such as calling on boys more often or gearing school activities more to the males.
3. Boys were found to call out answers eight times more often than girls. When boys call out, teachers are more apt to listen. A more common response when girls call out is "Raise your hand if you wish to speak."
4. When boys do not answer, teachers seem more likely to encourage them to give answers or opinions than to encourage girls.
5. Girls are sometimes at a disadvantage in taking tests because such tests may be geared to male performance. Taking this into account, some standard intelligence tests now have a masculinity-femininity index.
6. Although there does not appear to be much difference in test anxiety between girls and boys, at the same time girls are prone to suffer more stress over report cards than boys.
7. Teachers appear to encourage male students to work with laboratory equipment, especially in the more complex sciences. In one eleventh-grade class, an electric meter was used by 49 percent of the boys but only 17 percent of the girls. In that setting the teacher took no initiative to encourage or require that girls make meaningful use of the equipment.
8. Vocational education programs are often geared to boys in spite of the fact that a significant percent of the workforce is female.
9. Stereotypical images still appear in textbooks with, for example, an overwhelming number of male authors and role models studied in the class.

School systems are attempting to correct some of these conditions by inaugurating gender-equity and gender-neutral programs for motivation and instruction.

Stress is a highly individualized, subjective perception. One expert on the subject, Helen McCready Kearney[2] has raised the question: "Is there a commonality of stressors to which women are uniquely susceptible?" To this, the consensus is affirmative, as is the judgment that such stressors have multiplied at a rate far in excess of those of their male counterparts. This is attributed in large measure to radical changes in societal norms that have attended women's suffrage, the feminist movement, dramatic rates of divorce, increased geographical mobility, discontinuity in extended family relationships, and a steady influx of women into occupations and professions that were previously the proprietary interest and domains of males.

Among the negative consequences of such cultural transformations in the role of women have been disturbing qualitative and quantitative changes in illness patterns and increased incidence of life-threatening diseases among females. In fact, it was recently suggested that stress is causing more women than ever to consult their physicians; 50 percent of female office visits are said to be stress related, and twice as many women as men make such office visits.

A number of authors have suggested that there are signs that women's vulnerability to stress and physical illness increases at a pace in direct proportion to their newly achieved forms of employment opportunities and self-directed lifestyle.[3] In fact, it is claimed that a century ago, peptic ulcers were a woman's ailment, by a ratio of 7 to 3. Then, as frontier rigors were replaced gradually by those of the industrial age, life supposedly got easier for women, and more difficult and stressful for men—so that by the period from 1929 to 1940, nine out of ten new victims were male. But since mid-century, the incidence of ulcers in women was again on the rise (as well as the incidence of coronary disease). The meaning of these various studies and viewpoints are the basis of considerable debate in our society to this day.[4]

An interesting point of view was once expressed by Marianne Frankenhaeuser of the Experimental Psychology Research Unit of the Swedish Medical Research Council. She suggested that women do not have the same readiness as do men in responding to environmental demands by adrenaline release. She does not feel that this response is due to gender, but more so to role perception and behavior patterns that are common to men in Western society.[5]

A study of gender individual differences in stress reactivity is one that was conducted by Joy Humphrey and George Everly.[6] They used a "State Measurement Scale" to assess how male and female college students generally felt while experiencing a stress response situation. In other words, the purpose of the study was to investigate the perceptual dimensions of stress reactions in males and females.

The study demonstrated that males and females *perceive* different stress reactions. Of greatest disparity between the perceptions of males and females was the emergence of gastrointestinal sensitivities (such as upset stomach) exclusively among males and the emergence of an aversive affective sensitivity (such as feeling tense or "high strung") exclusively among females.

The investigators felt that it was impossible to attribute any overriding significance to the appearance of a gastrointestinal sensitivity among males and an affective sensitivity among females. However, they did surmise that sociocultural factors may have been involved. The reason for this is that it may be socially acceptable for males to develop what have been called "executive ulcers." Regarding the affective sensitivity, generally speaking, males are taught to repress emotions, and many males perceive such emotion to be a sign of weakness. Similarly, females have been traditionally taught that it is appropriate for them to demonstrate emotion. As this era of changing gender roles progresses it will be interesting to see if perceptions of stress responsiveness change as well. If cultural factors do indeed influence perceptions of responsiveness, one might be willing to speculate that, eventually, there would be more homogeneous perception of stress reactions among males and females.

Another indication that women could be generally more stressed than men is based on their prescription drug consumption. Drugs for psychological or mental conditions are prescribed twice as often for females as for males, but the reason for this is not clear.[7] One possibility is that women with emotional problems may be much more likely to consult a physician and also much more apt to admit that they are suffering from such difficulties than men who may have the same or similar conditions. On the other hand, epidemiologic studies suggest that members of the female gender are indeed more prone to anxiety and depressive disorders. Feminists counter by suggesting that the reason for this is that women are exploited in society and are therefore bound to suffer greater stress, which is mistakenly assumed by their (often male) doctors to produce intrinsic nervous instability. It is also posited that males in Western culture traditionally have vented their frustrations, anxieties, and anger through overt or aggressive behaviors more so than would be considered appropriate for females.

Finally, it is also suggested that because female physicians may be more sympathetic and understanding, they are able to diagnose anxiety states more accurately and frequently, and therefore regard drug therapy as appropriate treatment.[8]

Having explored the subject of female and male gender differences in those dimensions (a subject of considerable sensitivity and debate in contemporary society), we now move to the subject of stress among male and female student-athletes, with attention focused on the telling results of the survey and study.

CAUSES OF STRESS AMONG COLLEGE ATHLETES

Factors that induce stress are likely to be both general and specific in nature. As mentioned in Chapter 1, this means that certain major life events can be stress-inducing. Also, in our day-to-day environments, many specific concerns can elevate undesirable stress levels. Also, causes of stress may be peculiar to certain populations—in this case, college athletes.

Our responses to causes of stress from athletes were classified as: (a) academic problems, (b) athletics demands, (c) time, (d) relationships with others, and (e) finances.

In the area of academic problems, 95 percent of the male athletes and 86 percent of the female athletes were stressed by such factors as tests and examinations, preparing papers for classes, missing classes because of travel to athletics events, and making up missed assignments. One of the foremost stressors in this classification was the tests that students are required to take in the various subject areas— specifically, the preparation for those tests in the context of their physically and emotionally expending sports practices and competitions. As one NCAA Division I football player said, ". . . football practice and games are like hitting your head ten times against a brick wall and then you go try to study for a math exam."[9]

Also, test anxiety is a significant factor for all students, including student-athletes. In this regard, it is interesting to note that there is now an area of extensive psychological study known as test anxiety. Among other things, educators are trying to determine what the nature and scope of test anxiety implies for educational goals and practices.

For student-athletes, the time and the physical and mental energy needed to prepare for tests as well as other academic requirements were frequently cited as a serious problem for them because of the demands of their sport.

With regard to athletics demands, slightly more than half of the male athletes and 60 percent of the female athletes reported such demands as stress-inducing. By far the greatest stressor for athletes was the pressure put on them to win. Other stressors cited were exhausting and stressful practice sessions and distant travel to athletics contests.

Various factors related to time were serious causes of stress for more than 40 percent of the male athletes and well over half for the female athletes. Many said they were put under stress because of insufficient time for planning. Most of the respondents felt that there was not enough time to combine academics and athletics and to do their best in both areas.

Twelve percent of the male athletes and 7 percent of the female athletes were stressed by relationships with others. Included here were negative and unsatisfactory relationships with teachers, coaches, and fellow athletes.

Finally, 7 percent of both male and female athletes contended that finances (lack thereof) was a stressful concern. Practically all of these respondents were athletes who were not recipients of athletics grants.

CONSEQUENCES OF STRESS AMONG COLLEGE ATHLETES

We have already mentioned that stress can result in many serious health problems. This is especially true of prolonged and unrelenting stress that becomes chronic. Although not all young adult athletes are immediately at risk for serious stress-related conditions, there is some evidence that they could be affected in some way later in life. Also, we are well aware of some older adults who have vivid memories of a poor athletic performance that they have recalled and which has troubled them for years—and therefore has created stress for them over time.

We have identified consequences of stress among athletes as follows: (a) impact on mental/emotional health, (b) impact on physical health, (c) negative impact on athletic performance, and (d) negative impact on academic performance.

Almost half of the male athletes and slightly more than half of female athletes said that stress affected their mental/emotional health. They cited such factors as outbursts of anger, pressure to win, excessive anxiety, frustration, conflict, irritation, and fear.

As far as impact on physical health was concerned, about one in ten of the male athletes and about one in five of the female athletes mentioned such factors as not enough sleep, continuous tension, fatigue, headaches, and digestive problems.

Eleven percent of male athletes and 5 percent of female athletes said that stress negatively influenced athletic performance, mainly in terms of tension and being overanxious before and during participation. This was described often as being "uptight" or "too tight."

Twenty percent of male athletes and 14 percent of female athletes reported that stress had a negative impact on academic performance. They identified such factors as lower grades and not acquiring needed information as a result of missing classes because of team travel.

An unexpected but encouraging finding was that stress had a *positive* influence on a number of student-athletes. Ten percent of the male athletes and 9 percent of the female athletes indicated that they found stress to be a motivational factor. Also, almost one-third of the male athletes and one-fifth of the female athletes reported that they felt no ill effects from stress. However, some respondents suggested that a negative effect might have been present but that they might not have been aware of it.

COPING WITH STRESS
AMONG COLLEGE ATHLETES

To cope means to deal with and attempt to overcome challenges, problems, and difficulties. Generally speaking, stress coping procedures can be divided into the two broad categories of coping *behaviors* and coping *techniques.*

Coping Behaviors

As mentioned in Chapter 1, we will consider behavior as anything that the human body does as a result of some sort of stimulus. The coping behaviors that we have asked college athletes to respond to are termed *principles of living.* Obviously, no resolute standard behaviors are guaranteed to relieve a person entirely from undesirable stress. There are, however, certain general principles in the form of behaviors that may be applied as guidelines to help alleviate stressful conditions. Therefore, the following principles should be considered as guidelines, but not necessarily in any particular order of importance. In addition, it should be recognized that each principle is not a separate entity unto itself; all of the principles are in some way interrelated and interdependent upon each other. (The percent of male and female athletes who reported that they engaged in these behaviors is shown following each principle.)

Principle #1: Practice good personal health habits.
Males = 42 Percent, Females = 60 Percent

This is an easy principle to accept, but sometimes it is difficult to implement. This should not be difficult for athletes, at least in season, since they are expected to "keep in training" with regard to healthful nutrition, sleep habits, conditioning, and other factors. However, off-season behavior could differ markedly. A significant percentage of student-athletes indicated that this initiative or principle of practicing good health habits was an important way in which they coped with stress.

Principle #2: Learn to recognize and value
your own accomplishments.
Males = 42 Percent, Females = 33 Percent

One must learn to recognize his or her own accomplishments and praise oneself for them, especially if such praise is not offered by others. This is generally known as "stroking," or "patting oneself on the back." In practicing this procedure, positive attitudes and belief systems can be developed about one's accomplishments and thus reduce stress. The college athletes in the survey indicated that this life principle was helpful in managing stress when used sensibly.

Principle #3: Learn to take one thing at a time.
Males = 70 Percent, Females = 72 Percent

This principle is concerned with time budgeting and procrastination. As previously mentioned, the time factor can be stress inducing for student-athletes. Tasks need to be sorted out in order of importance and attacked one at a time. A high percentage of respondents used this principle effectively to cope with stress.

Principle #4: Learn to take things less seriously.
Males = 42 Percent, Females = 44 Percent

The athletes did not mean that schoolwork and athletics should not be taken seriously. They clearly understood that a fine line exists between what we sometimes deem to be serious or preeminently important, but may not be so. Sometimes when people look back at an event, they may wonder how they could have become so concerned about it. Many student-athletes indicated that they were attempting to keep these issues in balanced perspective in order to cope with stress.

Principle #5: Do things for others.
Males = 30 Percent, Females = 49 Percent

People can sometimes take their minds off their own stressful conditions by offering to do something for another person. When individuals help others to relieve stress, they in turn will tend to be relieved of stress. Research shows that those persons who volunteer to help others often get as much, if not more, benefit from this practice. Student-athletes in the survey indicated that they found this to be a healthy practice in dealing with stress.

Principle #6: Talk things over with others.
Males = 65 Percent, Females = 58 Percent

People often tend to keep things to themselves, and consequently, they may not be aware that others might be disturbed by the same stress-inducing factors. The experience of simply talking with someone about one's stress-inducing experiences tends to help dissipate stress. This universal principle is frequently used by the athletes surveyed. Often, discussing something with a fellow athlete or coach can help one see things in a much different perspective.

Coping Techniques

Surveys of various populations show that people use a variety of techniques to cope with stress. This was also true of the college athletes in our survey, as follows.

More than half of the male athletes and three-fourths of the female athletes engaged in physical exercise as a means of coping. This included exercise activities other than those required in athletics participation.

Recreational activities were used as coping techniques, with 66 percent of the male athletes and 63 percent of the female athletes engaging in such activities as reading, card playing, table games, video games, and other similar activities.

For several years the technique of muscle relaxation has been considered one of the most important stress reducers. Indeed, about one-fourth of both the male and female athletes practiced this procedure.

About 15 percent of both male and female athletes engaged in meditation, while less than 2 percent of all athletes used biofeedback. The latter technique has met with a great deal of success in reducing many stressful conditions. Perhaps its lack of use among college athletes is due to their unfamiliarity with this process. The above forms of stress reduction (muscle relaxation, meditation, and biofeedback) will be discussed in detail in subsequent chapters.

About one-fourth of the male athletes and 14 percent of the female athletes indicated faith in a practice of some form of divine guidance. This included prayer as well as reading various forms of religious literature such as the Bible, Talmud, or Koran for peace of mind and stress management.

A very disturbing finding was revealed in the use of alcoholic beverages as a means of coping with stress. Over one-half of the male athletes and about one-third of the female athletes engaged in this practice regularly.[10]

In this regard, recent studies show that drinking among college athletes as well as the general student population has increased dramatically in recent years. In fact, it has become one of the most challenging situations for college officials who try to deal with this increasing problem. One relevant question is: "Does regular drinking of alcoholic beverages *reduce* or *induce* stress?" Some studies suggest that acute or chronic exposure to low doses of alcohol may reduce the response to a stressor. However, some studies indicate that in some individuals at certain doses alcohol actually induces the stress response by stimulating hormone release by the hypothalamus, pituitary, and adrenal glands. In addition to the hormone stress response, chronic exposure to alcohol also results in an increase in adrenaline release into the circulatory system along with other mood-altering and physiological results.[11] The regular or chronic use of alcohol by young adults has serious negative implications for the individual practicing this technique.

Finally, in this chapter we have reviewed many of the issues involved in the subject of stress among college athletes. We have taken a careful look at gender differences and have profiled the causes, consequences, and the coping strategies of college athletes related to stress in their student-athlete experience.

Chapter 4

Stress Among Coaches
and Athletic Directors

In this chapter we will discuss those factors that are stressful concerns for coaches and athletic directors. Again, emphasis will be placed upon causes, consequences, and coping.

STRESS AMONG COACHES

As nearly as can be determined, the earliest recorded use of the term *coach* occurred somewhere around mid-nineteenth century. It was used in Great Britain to describe a tutor who conveyed a student through his examinations. It soon found use in this country and was defined as one who instructs players in the fundamentals of competitive sports and directs team strategy.[1]

The coaching profession is characterized by its uniqueness. A coach is at once a teacher, a psychologist, a father/mother figure, and various other roles that he or she finds it expedient or necessary to assume at a given time.

Clearly, the college athletics coach labors in a stressful environment. It is a volatile and sometimes unpredictable profession with numerous and concurrent pressures. These include the need to continuously interact personally and effectively with his or her student-athletes regarding myriads of training, competitive, academic, and personal issues; the pressure to recruit and develop a winning team; and the need to handle defeat. Over a period of time, the coach is faced with his or her own vulnerability.

The essence of coaching is the balance between being caring, motivational, supportive, and approachable, while maintaining the firm discipline and uncompromising determination to require of student-athletes the academic and competitive excellence that also characterizes outstanding college coaches. Indeed, effective human relations are as important to a coach's success as his or her command of the game itself. Clearly, coaching demands many more competencies than just being able to teach a specific skill. And it is possible that some coaches may not be able to cope with the physical and emotional exhaustion resulting from demands on their energy, emotions, and time. At the same time, coaching as a profession can be as personally compelling and enjoyable as it can be frustrating and difficult. Successful coaches accept the rigors of their profession while recognizing their strengths and weaknesses. Although they are constantly striving for improvement and growth, they also accept who they are and, as a result, they remain productive, balanced, and successful throughout their coaching careers.

Causes of Stress

We obtained from coaches themselves those factors that induced the most stress, its consequences, and how they cope with it. This was accomplished by simply requesting that they identify those factors connected with their job that were most stressful for them. Obviously, this resulted in a large mass of data. It seemed appropriate to sort out the stressors and place them in what appeared to be the most appropriate classifications.

As mentioned previously, the difficulty encountered in attempting to devise a seamless system for the classification of coaches' stressors lies in the fact that it is sometimes not possible to fit an identified stressor into one exclusive classification because of the incidence of overlapping. However, an attempt was made to do so and the results indicate that the classifications are representative of the kinds of responses received from coaches. Others might wish to use different classifications than those used here, and in the absence of anything resembling standardization, it would be their prerogative to do so. With this idea in mind, the following classifications of coaches' stressors were identified:

1. Players
2. Performance
3. Outside Influences
4. Time

5. Associates
6. Public Relations
7. Finances

Players

There is no question that those who participate on an athletics team are its most important asset. Anyone knows that without the proper material (adequate player personnel) coaches would not be able to consistently produce competitively successful teams. But many coaches are in the profession because of the personal satisfaction they derive from dealing with the young men and women with whom they are associated, whatever their skill level.

It is not uncommon for coaches to refer to team members and others closely associated with them as a "family." And, even though in most families the members love and respect one another, at the same time they can be stressful to one another. So it is not surprising that players can be a stress-inducing factor for coaches. Indeed, in this stress classification (players), 85 percent of the coaches reported sources of stress. These stressors are identified in the following subclassifications.

Player behavior and attitude. This was a serious stressor for coaches, with 38 percent of the player stressors in this category. Among the things that stressed coaches the most in regard to player behavior and attitude were:

- Apathy and indifference of players
- Social problems such as the requirement for drug testing
- Players behaving improperly or unlawfully on campus and in town
- Insubordination of players
- Dissensions among players
- Selfishness of players
- Any kind of team conflict
- Players not accepting responsibility for their own actions
- Lack of maturity of players
- Players who do not consider the best interest of the team

Recruiting. It is not surprising that 22 percent of player stressors are found in this category. Coaches were not only stressed by the general aspect of recruiting, but some specific aspects were:

- Failing to get the top athletes
- Not getting your quota of recruits
- The last two days of recruiting are especially stressful
- Rejecting people who expect to be recruited

Academic performance of players. Seventeen percent of the player stressors were in this category. It is well-known that numerous troubling and even scandalous incidents in college athletics have been related to academic issues. Among the stressors for coaches were:

- Players not interested in graduating
- The stress of keeping players eligible to participate
- Players failing to progress academically
- Cheating on examinations or otherwise receiving fraudulent grades

Player performance. Coaches are concerned about how their players perform and 15 percent of the stressors were in this category. Among the most important were:

- Players not performing to their potential
- Not getting the best effort or attitude from his or her players
- Difficulty in motivating players to perform
- Excuses of players for not performing well
- Lack of dedication and commitment of players

Injuries. Coaches worry about injuries to players—both in regard to the success of the team and their feelings and concern for their players. Eight percent of the stressors were in this category and, as might be expected, the majority of concerns regarding injury were among football coaches.

Performance

This category of stressors pertains to the performance of the coach. In this classification, a notable 78.5 percent of the coaches reported sources of stress. This classification overlaps to some extent with performance of players, but for the most part involved the coach's own feelings about his or her ability and performance. No attempt was made to make subclassification because of the difficulty in doing so. Examples of stressors in this classification include:

- Inability to produce consistently winning teams
- Game day performance
- Losing games that should have been won
- Not winning the "big game"
- Losing games on chance factors or circumstances that were perceived as beyond the control of the coach
- Waiting for the kickoff before a game
- High expectations not met
- Game day participation/performance of coach

Outside Influences

Included here is any individual who is outside the immediate group of team members, coaches, and others who have a close working relationship such as trainers, managers, chaplains, and team physicians. A remarkable 54 percent of the coaches reported stressors in this classification. Included among such stressors were:

- Reactions of alumni and other fans
- Not being able to please administrators
- Officiating
- Hate mail
- NCAA rules and policies
- Dealing with unqualified people trying to run my job
- Things that are controlled by others
- Criticism that is unwarranted
- Outside influences on athletes such as drugs, alcohol, and agents
- Faculty members who do not accept the values of athletics in the total university program

Time

In most studies of occupational stress conducted by Humphrey, well over one-fourth of the respondents cite factors related to time as serious causes of stress. One-half of this number cite insufficient time for planning and about one-third cite not enough time in the day to do the job expected of them. Notably, 41 percent of the coaches reported stressors in this classification. Such stressors included:

- Not having enough time for family
- Not enough time to get everything done
- Time and priority allocations
- Abundance of time-consuming travel required
- Meeting deadlines
- Not enough time for players' needs

Associates

Success in any endeavor, coaching included, depends upon the cooperation of group members. In the present context associates are identified as the assistants to the head coach. It was surprising to find that 32 percent of the coaches reported this classification as a cause of stress.

Most coaches maintain firm control and good relationships in their dealings with staff members, but according to our findings, this is not always the case. In fact, one coach made this statement: "Much stress is created by groups within the staff itself. Selfishness is a key to stressful situations. The less selfishness within the staff, the less stressful situations are seen." The following were most stressful in this category:

- Getting personalties of the program to work together
- Unpleasant interpersonal relationships with staff
- Treating conflicts among staff members
- Lack of communication with staff
- Staff placing their recruits ahead of needs of the team
- Motives of associates

- Motivating staff
- Hiring and maintaining a stable staff

Public Relations

Twenty-one percent of the coaches reported some aspect of public relations as being stressful. The stressors were related to the areas identified by these coaches in their following statements:

- Misunderstanding by the media and public
- Lack of media understanding and printing the truth
- Media innuendo
- Dealing with time demands of the media
- Dealing with time demands of the public
- Being in public after losing a game

Finances

A majority of coaches believe that the financing of athletics programs is mainly the responsibility of others and only 12 percent of them reported this classification as a source of stress. A few coaches indicated that they felt stress due to the lack of money for their programs and others said they were under stress to win in order to finance other sports.

The preceding discussion of the data on stress-inducing factors was presented as an aggregate to include all coaches who provided responses. At this point it seems appropriate to cite these comparative data for female coaches and male coaches. The information in Table 4.1 is provided for this purpose.

TABLE 4.1. Comparison of Stressors for Female and Male Coaches

Stress Classification	Percent for Females	Percent for Males
Players	90	83
Performance	90	67
Outside Influences	50	58
Time	50	33
Associates	23	41
Public Relations	11	31
Finances	10	13

It would be speculative at best to offer reasons for the differences between women and men coaches. Each reader will interpret the results individually. However, we would comment on the significant difference in the stressor classification of public relations. We have discussed this with selected female coaches who believe that they generally do not have enough media attention nor sufficiently pervasive or vigorous public interest for these sources to create significant stress. (It is possible that indeed this *lack* of attention for their sport could be a potential stressor for some females. Again, however, this would be speculation since the study did not focus on this issue.)

Consequences of Stress

The effect that stress has on coaches can be classified into the following two broad areas: (a) impact on physical health, and (b) impact on mental/emotional health.

Forty-seven percent of the coaches perceived an impact on their physical health while more than half said that stress affected their mental/emotional health. The following statements by some coaches indicate physical effects:

- It affects me physically with loss of sleep.
- Stress will have an influence on my eating habits and sleeping.
- Very often stress causes me to have an upset stomach.

Regarding affect on mental/emotional health, some coaches commented as follows:

- Sometimes I have an emotional outburst against the team and I hate myself for it after it is over.
- I get terribly frustrated when I lose and it takes me too long to get over it.
- It causes me to get angry with no really good reason for it.

Only about 10 percent of the coaches said that stress did not bother them. They made such comments as:

- Stress in coaching can be handled with a systematic daily routine of spiritual nourishment; therefore it does not bother me.

- Stress is greatly overrated. If you are organized and have a plan you should not be stressed.
- I never feel any stress in coaching; however, maybe I experience it but don't know that I'm experiencing it.

Coping Behaviors

Regarding the coping behaviors inherent in the principles of living, the following results were apparent.

Principle #1: Practicing good personal health habits.

The imposing workload of a coach may cause him or her to neglect the basic requirements that are essential for the human being to maintain an adequate functional health level. (Recall how stress had an effect on the physical health of some coaches.) Fifty-two percent of the coaches said they abided by this principle. Thus, almost half of them neglect some aspect of their personal health.

Principle #2: Learn to recognize and value
your own accomplishments.

Sometimes coaches do not accept or assume enough credit for their own performance and achievements. (See previous comment under *performance* as a cause of stress for coaches.) Thirty-three percent of the coaches said that they practiced this principle of valuing their own achievements.

Principle #3: Learn to take one thing at a time.

Some coaches are likely to put things off, especially unpleasant things, and, as a consequence, frustrations can build as tasks pile up. An important solution to this for coaches is the practice of taking one task or problem at a time. We are all familiar with coaches who talk about "taking one game at a time." Budgeting of time can also help eliminate serious worries related to time urgency and the feeling of "too much to do in too short a time." Sixty-three percent of the coaches indicated that they practiced this principle to diminish the stress under which they were functioning.

Principle #4: Learn to take things less seriously.

Often a coach will take the loss of a game too seriously. It is important to remember this single truism: A game that has been lost can never be won no matter how much a coach may fret or agonize over it. Those coaches who are able to keep the challenges of their profession and specific losses in perspective and to see the humorous side of various situations, tend to look at a potentially stressful situation more objectively. Clearly, this can assist in keeping stress levels lower. Forty-seven percent of the coaches said they abide by this principle.

Principle #5: Do things for others.

It can be stated unequivocally that most coaches try to do a considerable amount on behalf of their players. That in itself, as well as other acts of assisting individuals in some way, can help to relieve coaches from stress. Generally, this is a principle of human nature. Forty percent of the coaches said that they practiced this principle to relieve stress.

Principle #6: Talk things over with others.

One coach commented that it would be a good idea for coaches to get together to have a dialogue about the stressful conditions of the profession. It is important to keep in mind that such discussion should best be positive and objective lest it degenerate into idle gossip. Of course there is value sometimes in simply venting frustrations or fears regarding challenges, problems, and issues. Three-fourths of the coaches said they practiced this principle and in most instances they talked issues over with family members or close friends.

Coping Techniques

Coaches were asked to identify the techniques they used in attempting to deal with stress. Three techniques that are specifically used for inducing a relaxation response—*muscle relaxation, meditation,* and *biofeedback* were used; as well as the techniques of *physical exercise, recreational activities, resorting to divine guidance,* and *consumption of alcoholic beverages.*

The three techniques for inducing a relaxation response were as follows: 17 percent used muscle relaxation, 3 percent used meditation, and less than 1 percent used biofeedback. As mentioned previously, all of these techniques are discussed in detail in subsequent chapters and recommendations are made as to how they might be applied to relieve stress in coaches and athletic administrators.

Eighty-six percent of the coaches engaged in physical exercise as a means of reducing stress. However, most said that this was done more or less sporadically.

Nearly half of the respondents said they engaged in recreational activities, including such activities as reading, card games, and listening to music.

Slightly more than half of the coaches resorted to divine guidance and the following are representative statements in this regard:

- In dealing with stress, I put my faith in God.
- A personal commitment to Christ is my central theme, and the only way I have been able to lessen stress.
- When I feel stressed I personally draw peace and strength from my relationship with the Lord.

Ten percent of the coaches said they used alcohol with some regularity in order to cope with the stress of their work.

Simply stated, individuals dealing with the problems of stress differ, techniques for dealing with stress differ, and what might be successful for one person might not be necessarily so for another.

Finally, the information presented in Tables 4.2 and 4.3 is intended to make comparisons of female and male coaches in terms of the procedures they use to cope with stress.

Again, the reader is left to his or her own judgment regarding the reasons for the differences. It is not entirely clear which of the sexes in the coaching profession is more sensitive to or susceptible to stress reactivity, or which of the interventions are most useful. In the absence of completely objective evaluative criteria, such questions will remain difficult to answer.

What is very clear is that coaches function under considerable stress and that among a significant percentage of college coaches this stress is pervasive and almost unrelenting. In February 1999 the Iowa State Legislature presented the University of Iowa's retiring

TABLE 4.2 Comparison of Female and Male Coaches in the Application of Principles of Living to Avoid Stress

Principle	Percent for Females	Percent for Males
Observing personal health practices	45	60
Recognizing your own accomplishments	27	40
Taking one thing at a time	67	60
Taking things less seriously	45	48
Doing things for others	45	36
Talking things over with others	78	72

TABLE 4.3. Comparison of Female and Male Coaches for Specific Stress-Reducing Techniques

Technique	Percent for Females	Percent for Males
Physical Exercise	91	84
Recreational Activities	36	56
Muscle Relaxation	18	16
Meditation	2.4	3.6
Biofeedback	0.2	0.4
Divine Guidance	55	56
Use of Alcohol	8	12

head football coach, Hayden Fry, with a ceremony and resolution of appreciation for his eighteen years of service to the institution and the state. Coach Fry's final season had ended several weeks before, but one of his compelling statements at the ceremony was, "I'm trying to learn how to relax."[2] Coaches across the profession would understand his statement—after eighteen excellent years at Iowa, following his successful years at Southern Methodist University and previous experiences. Clearly, it was only after he was out from under the unrelenting stress of the coaching profession that he was at last finding an opportunity ". . . to relax."

Accountability for Student-Athlete Welfare

One notable current movement in the NCAA is the viable and pervasive emphasis on student-athlete welfare. Among the several emphases of this movement are the physical, academic, and personal welfare of the college athlete. This trend represents an important recognition of the accountability that the athletics department, the institution, and the coaching staff must accept to assure that in every way possible each athlete will be viewed as a person of value and importance beyond the court and playing field—that they are worthy of everyone's best effort to see that they develop and succeed at all levels as an individual and as a student.

For decades, great coaches have accepted this role and this accountability. In July 1954, coach Brutus Hamilton, track coach at the University of California at Berkeley, wrote a recruiting letter to an outstanding high school runner named Don Bowden. It reflected his commitment to the welfare and total development of the student-athlete and his commitment to "coaching the whole person":[3]

> There is not much I can add to what I told you when you last visited the campus. You know pretty well what kind of a coach I am, since we have visited together and since you heard me speak at your meeting there in San Jose. You know our facilities, our schedule, and you know the prestige of the university as an educational institution. There can be no degree more coveted than one earned here. I think you know, too, that we have a healthy attitude toward sports here at Berkeley. We want our boys to win; we want them to maximize their potentialities in sports, but *we don't want them doing so at the expense of the more serious phases of college life* [italics added]. Your principal purpose in going to college, of course, is to get an education in your field of study which will probably be medicine. If you can break the world's record in the half-mile, which seems quite likely to me, while doing this, well and good. The main thing, however, is to be graduated a capable, self-reliant young man which your parents and friends want you to be. I can assure you that we here in the Athletic Department will do everything possible to see that your goals are achieved.

Don Bowden enrolled at the University of California at Berkeley, was a successful student, and became the first American to run the mile in under four minutes (on June 1, 1957).

Likewise, in 1999 the head football coach at the University of Maryland expressed his commitment to the welfare of his student-athletes when he said, "I measure my success not solely by our wins on the field, but also by our young men winning in the classroom and in life. That is our firm and uncompromising goal and we will not settle for less" (Coach Ron Vanderlinden, College Park, Maryland, press conference, February 1999).

The kind of accountability embraced by these and many other college coaches clearly adds to the scope of responsibility and the stress of the profession, but they indicate that it also presents an opportunity for the job of coaching to take on a more meaningful and personal dimension.

STRESS AMONG ATHLETIC DIRECTORS

The position of the college athletic director is similar in a number of ways to that of a corporate chief executive officer. That is, among a host of other duties, the director performs such functions as management of finances, supervising the implementation of policies, conducting public relations, and addressing personnel issues.

Athletic directors in our nationwide survey were from colleges and universities ranging in enrollment from several hundred to several thousand students. In this regard, a recent study by Copeland and Kirsch[4] at all levels of enrollment is of interest. These researchers believed that increasing demands among contemporary administrators of intercollegiate athletics may potentially create role overload and lead to significant occupational stress. The purpose of the study was to identify perceived levels of intrinsic administrative tasks among NCAA Divisions I, II, and III athletic directors and to determine if these perceptions varied by divisional status. A twenty-one-item survey was administered to randomly selected athletic directors to assess (a) demographics, (b) general perceptions of occupational stress, and (c) levels of task-related stress on a five-point scale. Among the findings were: (a) there were no significant differences in general perceptions of job stress across divisions; (b) significant differences were revealed for task-related stress between Division I and II in policy decision making, and in Division II and III in regard to fund-raising; and (c) budget demands and dismissing employees rated highest as *almost always* stressful across divisions. Thus, it could be concluded that regardless of the size of the program administered, there are some similarities of stress reactivity experienced by athletic directors.

(Note: We should mention that less than 6 percent of our sample of athletic directors were women. Therefore, it is not practical to try to compare the responses of men and women as we were able to do with athletes and coaches.)

Causes of Stress

The greatest stress-inducing factors for athletic directors were classified into the following four categories:

1. Finances
2. Personnel
3. Outside Influences
4. Public Relations

Finances

Whereas only 12 percent of coaches cited finances as a stress-inducing factor, three-fourths of the athletic directors found their financial problems to be extremely stressful. Not only do they have the responsibility for equitable distribution of available funds, but at the same time they may be expected to be very active in the soliciting of those funds. The following are athletic directors' comments regarding the stressfulness of their financial situations:

- Too many difficult issues are related to balancing budgets and this creates continuous financial pressure
- Having to finance programs that do not generate any income
- Winning and losing in revenue sports that leads to serious revenue concerns
- Rising costs without rising income
- Never enough income to balance the budget
- Trying to reduce large capital debts
- Increasing costs because of Title IX

- Budget problems are a real challenge and a losing battle
- The impossible task of properly funding all programs
- Competing with other entertainment areas for the dollar
- Fiscal control in terms of short- and long-term financial management
- The added responsibility of trying to raise additional funds

Personnel

More than two-thirds of the athletic directors considered personnel issues to be significantly stressful.

In an extensive study,[5] one of the authors collected data on *boss types* (those individuals who were an employee's immediate supervisor). Included in the study were all manner of managers, including those who held the highest level executive positions. Consistently, one of the most significant stressors for bosses was incompetent workers. Other stress-inducing factors for them were not too unlike those identified by those they supervised. They felt plagued by a multitude of daily interruptions that deterred them from completing tasks that they had started. Another stressful condition was unexpected situations that prevented them from being able to block out time to plan or execute an intended plan. Many found it stressful when they had to reorganize priorities almost daily. Also stress inducing were too many meetings and too many matters to coordinate simultaneously.

Another study[6] of forty-nine executives revealed that they were worried or tense more than twice as much when they were at work than at other times, and that they were under significant stress almost 70 percent of the time during the workday. Those who had greatest stress levels reported about four times more complaints of physical/health problems and illnesses and had a much higher incidence of psychological problems such as anxiety and depression. Perhaps such findings could apply to athletic directors as well.

Some ways in which personnel factors caused stress for athletic directors, again in their own words, were as follows:

- Dealing with situations with little factual information and lack of cooperation of staff members
- Misconduct of coaches

- Dismissing personnel because of lack of funds
- Internal conflict because of lack of cooperation
- Personnel who fail to produce
- Poor relationships with some coaches
- Lack of staff to meet the goals, demands, and personal expectations for the program
- Dealing with staff members who are not truthful
- Dealing with staff members with conflicting objectives
- Being responsible for the actions of staff members when I have virtually no control over them
- Personnel who try to interfere with management issues
- Actions by others for which I will be held accountable
- Coaches' requests and demands
- Administering uncooperative coaches
- Managing uncooperative staff
- When the football or basketball coach you hire is not successful

Outside Influences

Thirty-one percent of the athletic directors indicated that outside influences are a cause of stress, citing such issues as:

- Serious concerns about what I might not know about the involvement of agents, gambling interests, and boosters with our student-athletes
- Trying to satisfy the multiple publics of athletics such as boosters, alumni, university community, fans, or parents of players
- Others in and around athletics who want to be empowered but not enlightened
- Competitive/winning issues related to fans and alumni expectations
- Dealing with campus bureaucracy and a lack of "team" play on campus
- Dealing with faculty and administration who do not understand athletics and are jealous
- Potential compliance issues
- Dealing with power politics and political controversy

- Unexpected challenges caused by others not being accountable
- Interference from boosters, legislators, and university administrators when they do not have a real clue about how an athletics department is supposed to be run
- Unreasonable scrutiny and performance expectations from
  those who don't understand the problems

Public Relations

Ten percent of the athletic directors felt stress from issues related
to public relations. It is clear that athletic directors are often profoundly impacted by the exposure they have to the numerous publics of intercollegiate athletics. They were stressed by these issues
they described below:

- Public speaking after a losing season
- Excessive media scrutiny
- Media types who think they know all the answers
- Educating the public after it has formed its own opinion
- News reporters who make "pests" of themselves
- Satisfying everyone from members of the state legislature, to
  powerful alumni, to the boosters and fans, to the university
  president, to the NCAA, to parents of hundreds of student-
  athletes, etc.
- Media people who take up my time with [trivial questions]
- Dealing with corporate sponsors who have increasingly high
  expectations
- Trying to satisfy the general public
- The continuous and seemingly endless meetings and dinners
  with external and internal groups

Consequences of Stress

The effects of stress on athletic directors were considered in the
same two classifications as that of coaches. That is, impact on
physical health and mental/emotional health. There were 42 percent
whose physical health was impacted by stress and 48 percent per-

ceived that there were effects of stress on their mental/emotional health. Some statements about physical health were:

- I have an adverse physical reaction to the excessive pressure of work.
- I feel tired and overworked.
- I suffer from sleeplessness, making me too tired to exercise.
- I have difficulty sleeping and no appetite.
- I am wondering how my body will hold up under the same daily routine.
- It is bad for my physical health.
- It impacts my sleep on occasions and I tend to overeat.
- It can affect my sleep, diet and overall health.
- The unending series of games, events, travel, and the internal and external group meetings wears me down physically.
- It causes fatigue that infringes on other nonwork forms of activity.

Some of the statements made by athletic directors with regard to mental/emotional health were:

- Stress impacts my ability to think creatively due to mental fatigue.
- It puts a mental strain on me because I cannot do things that people ask of me.
- It inhibits my ability to make good decisions.
- It affects my ability to work effectively with others.
- Sometimes it is very upsetting for me.
- It can impact my peace of mind.
- I have mood swings, lots of anxiety, and at times feel frustrated and helpless.
- Sometimes I become quite irritated and impatient.
- I get filled with worry, anxiety, and tension.

Sixteen percent of the athletic directors did not believe that stress was a problem for them. Some of them commented as follows:

- I use stress to help me get a perspective on what is really important in life.
- I do not let stress overtake me—focus is the key.

- Sometimes I am energized by stressful situations and work at a higher level of proficiency.
- I don't feel I have a stressful job. I felt far more self-induced stress as a coach.

Coping with Stress

We have already commented on certain principles of living as behavioral means of dealing with stress. Therefore, we will simply list these principles here along with the percentage of athletic directors who indicated that they practiced these principles.

- Practice good personal health habits—3 percent
- Learn to value/recognize your own accomplishments—21 percent
- Learn to take on one thing at a time—60 percent
- Learn to take things less seriously—62 percent
- Do things for others—26 percent
- Talk things over with others—55 percent

With regard to the use of coping techniques, 64 percent engaged in physical exercise, 33 percent participated in recreational activities, 12 percent used muscle relaxation, 13 percent used meditation, 33 percent resorted to divine guidance, 2 percent used biofeedback, and, finally, 7 percent used alcoholic beverages to attempt to reduce stress.

Finally, in 1994 the executive search firm of Eastman and Beaudine conducted a survey of presidents of NCAA Division IA institutions in order to identify the skills, experiences, and characteristics that these presidents seek in athletic directors.[7] The results of the survey clearly postures the scope and complexity of the contemporary athletic director position. The desired profile was as follows:

1. Strategic thinking and the ability to lead in the formulation, implementation and evaluation of a viable strategic plan
2. Knowledge of and sensitivity to gender equity and other regulatory procedures
3. Ability to manage complex financial issues and budgets
4. Capability to direct a large and diverse staff, including coaches

5. Marketing expertise
6. Strong public speaking, writing, and media relations skills
7. Creativity and problem-solving abilities
8. Effective human resource talents for dealing with parents, students, faculty, booster groups, and sponsors

Added to these characteristics are the skills needed to supervise the important and pervasive academic issues that are an integral part of the work of a contemporary director of athletics.

In summary, as in the case of all successful executives, athletic directors should learn to *flow with their stress* when they perceive that challenges might represent opportunities that are within their capabilities to achieve, thus allowing them to utilize their time and talents optimally. Anxiety occurs when challenges are significant in nature, but only limited ability is present. Conversely, the combination of low challenges and low skills often results in apathy. Low challenges and high skills lead to boredom. Flow results when challenges and skills are high and are realistically matched to talent and time.

Chapter 5

Dealing with Emotions
in College Athletics

The athletics environment is replete with emotionally charged events, issues, and situations. These involve coaches, student-athletes, athletic administrators, and others within the athletics program. These also encompass the parents of athletes, fans, alumni, sports media types, and other groups and individuals in and around college athletics programs. The exhilaration, disappointment, fear, joy, and pathos that are integral functions of this frequently emotional environment contribute to the sheer drama of the athletics enterprise. How often have we heard a passionately contested event or recruiting battle referred to as "a game of emotion"? Frequently, no doubt. How often does the future of a college athletics team seem to rest on the impending and intensely awaited decision of a seventeen-year-old high school star athlete? Frequently we read of the athletics department that is being investigated by its governing body (NCAA or other). Consequently, the department, its boosters and fans, and the institution of which the athletics department is a part must cope with the embarrassing and sometimes seemingly debilitating results of such an investigation. These and many other scenarios indicate the emotion that is intrinsic to athletics programs.

Because of the emotion and passion that typically permeate intercollegiate athletics, individuals involved in all aspects of college athletics need to understand the complex nature of the phenomenon of human emotion. The purpose of this chapter is to discuss this phenomenon and thus provide useful information for understanding and dealing with emotional stress.

In discussing the subject of emotion, we are confronted with the fact that for decades emotion has been a difficult concept to define.

In addition, theories and ideas have changed repeatedly regarding the nature and scope of human emotion. In Chapter 1 we described emotion as the response an individual makes when confronted with a situation for which he or she is unprepared or which he or she interprets as a possible source of gain or loss.

Clearly, it is not the purpose of this book to attempt to explore in great scientific depth psychological and sociological implications of human emotion. However, a general overview of the subject will be in order with regard to the emotional dimension of college athletics, particularly regarding its relationship to stress.

Emotional stress can be induced by the stimulus of any of the human emotional precursors or responses. For example, the emotional pattern of anger can be stimulated by such factors as the thwarting of one's wishes, or the cumulative effects of a number of other disappointments and irritations. Response to such stimuli can be either *impulsive* or *inhibited*. Impulsive anger is directed toward an object or a person. The impulsive basketball coach may kick a chair (object) or vent his or her anger toward the referee (person) at the risk of being charged with a technical foul. Inhibited anger is kept under control and may be manifested by such overt behaviors as skin flushing, gritting of teeth and facial expressions. Witness the inhibited coach who sits with relative calmness on the bench, but we do not know what is going on inside his or her mind and his or her body.

Generally speaking, emotional patterns can be placed into the two broad psychological categories of *pleasant* and *unpleasant*. Pleasant emotional patterns include such things as joy, affection, and happiness. Included among the unpleasant emotional patterns are anger, sorrow, jealousy, fear, and worry—an imaginary form of fear.

It is interesting to note that a significant amount of the literature on this subject is devoted to emotions that are unpleasant. It has been found that, in a majority of basic psychology books, more space is given to such emotional patterns as fear, hate, and guilt, than to such pleasant emotional patterns as love, sympathy, joy, and contentment.

At one time or another most persons involved in college athletics (athletes, coaches, athletic directors, and others) have manifested overt emotional behavior as well as more restrained behavior. Differences in the structure of the human body (individual differences) and the environment will largely govern the degree to which one expresses emotional behavior. In addition, it has been suggested that the pleasantness or unpleasantness of an emotion seems to be determined by its strength or intensity, by the nature of the situation arousing it, and by the way the individual perceives or interprets the situation.

The ancient Greeks identified emotions with certain organs of the body. In general, sorrow was expressed from the heart (for example, a broken heart); jealousy was associated with the liver; hate with the gallbladder; and anger with the spleen (thus the observation that a coach was "venting his spleen" on the referee). We make this historical reference because in modern times we acknowledge certain conduits or connections between the emotions and the body via the nervous system and the endocrine system. The part of the nervous system principally concerned with the emotions is the autonomic nervous system, which controls functions such as heartbeat, blood pressure, and digestion. When there is a stimulus of any of the emotional patterns, these two systems activate in the manner explained previously. To illustrate this, if the emotional pattern of fear is stimulated, the heartbeat accelerates, breathing is more rapid, and blood pressure is likely to rise. Energy fuel is discharged into the blood from storage in the liver, which causes the blood sugar level to rise. These, along with other bodily functions, serve to prepare the person to cope with the condition caused by the fear. He or she then reacts with the fight or flight response that was discussed previously.

When we attempt to evaluate the emotional dimension of personality, we encounter various degrees of difficulty because of specific uncontrollable factors. The following are among the methods used to measure emotional responses:

1. *Blood pressure.* It rises when one experiences emotional stress.
2. *Blood sugar analysis.* Under stressful conditions, more sugar enters the blood stream.

3. *Galvanic skin response.* Similar to the lie detector technique, but with measurements recorded in terms of perspiration on the palms of the hands.
4. *Heart rate.* Emotional stress causes it to elevate. Later in this chapter we will discuss how heart rate of coaches is accelerated due to emotional reactivity during game conditions.

These measures can have various degrees of validity. In attempting to assess emotional reactivity, we often encounter the problem of the extent to which we are dealing with a purely physiological response or a purely emotional response. For example, one's heart rate could be elevated by participating in some sort of physical exercise. As we shall see later, it could also be elevated when a coach is in an emotional state during a tense game situation. Therefore, in this illustration, the elevation of heart rate could be caused for different reasons, the first being physiological and the second emotional. Also, the *type* of emotional pattern is not identified by the measuring device. A joy response and anger response will likely show the same or nearly the same rise in heart rate. These are a few of the reasons why it is often difficult to establish a high degree of objectivity in studying the emotional aspect of personality.

FACTORS RELATED TO EMOTIONAL STABILITY

Coaches, athletic directors, and athletes are involved in various kinds of experiences that are characterized by the necessity to make physical and psychological adjustments to sometimes unpredictable and often stressful circumstances. It could be said that normal behavior is the result of successful adjustment, and abnormal behavior results from unsuccessful adjustment. The degree of emotional adjustment that an individual involved in athletics achieves depends upon how adequately he or she is able to satisfy basic needs and to fulfill expectations within the environment—and also by the pattern or ways dictated by the individual situations that occur within that environment.

As mentioned earlier, stress may be considered as any factor acting internally or externally that renders adaptation difficult, and which induces increased effort on the part of the person to maintain a state of equilibrium within himself or herself and his or her environment. As suggested before, when stress is induced as a result of the individual's not being able to meet needs (basic demands) and satisfy desires (wants and wishes), *frustration* and *conflict* result. In Chapter 2, we indicated that frustration occurs when a need is not met and that conflict results when choices must be made between nearly equally attractive alternatives or when basic emotional forces oppose one another. In the emotionally healthy person, the degree of frustration ordinarily is in proportion to the intensity of the need or desire. That is, he or she will objectively observe and evaluate the situation to ascertain whether a solution is possible and, if so, what solution would best enable him or her to achieve the fulfillment of needs or desires. However, every person has a *zone of tolerance* or limits for emotional stress within which he or she normally operates. If the stress becomes considerably greater than the tolerance level, or if the individual has not learned to cope with his or her problems and objectively and intelligently solve them, some degree of temporary or permanent maladjustment will almost always result.

It could be said that the major difference between a normal person and a violent criminal confined to prison is that the normal person has the ability to control emotional impulses to a greater degree than the criminal. Perhaps many of us at one time or another have experienced the same kinds of emotions that have led the abnormally responding individual to commit violence, but we have been able to hold our powerful and abnormal emotions in check. This may be an extreme example, but it should suggest something of the importance of emotional control in modern society.

An important aspect of controlling the emotions is a person's ability to function effectively and rationally in an emotionally charged situation. Success in many life situations hinges upon this ability. This is particularly true in the athletics environment. Extremes of emotional upset must be avoided if the individual is to be able to think and act effectively. Making or missing a field goal in the NCAA basketball tournament could mean, among many other possible results, the loss of tens of thousands of dollars if a team advances or fails to advance to the next tournament round. And that is an emotionally charged situation for coaches and athletic directors, as well as players.

It is sometimes helpful to visualize your emotions as being forces within you that are in a struggle with your mind (and your capacity for deliberate reasoning) to control your actions/reactions. Sometimes, our basic emotions are blind and unconcerned with the welfare of other people, even with our own welfare. Emotional stability has to do with gaining increased mastery over our emotions, not eliminating them, so that we may behave as intelligent, rational, and civilized human beings.

To pursue a sensible course in our efforts to acquire desired emotional stability, certain factors need to be considered: (a) characteristics of emotionality, (b) emotional arousals and reactions, and (c) factors that influence emotionality.

Characteristics of Emotionality

Length of Emotions Vary

A child's emotions may last for a few minutes or less and then terminate rather abruptly. The child gets it "out of his system," so to speak, by expressing it outwardly. In contrast, adult emotions may be more protracted and constant. As children get older, expressing the emotions by overt action is encumbered by certain social restraints. This is to say that what might be socially acceptable at one age level is not necessarily so at another. This may be the reason why some children develop moods, which in a sense are states of emotion drawn out over a period of time and expressed slowly. Typical moods may be "sulking" due to restraint of anger, and being "jumpy" from repressed fear. Of course, it is common for these moods to prevail well into adulthood.

Differences in Intensity of Emotions

You will probably recall in your own experience that some persons may react rather strongly or even violently to a situation that, to you, might appear insignificant. The difference in the intensity of reactivity is influenced by one's background, past experience with specific kinds of situations, and genetic makeup.

Emotions Are Subject to Rapid Change

A young child is capable of shifting quickly from laughing to crying, or from anger to joy. Although the reason for this is not definitely known, it might be that not as much depth of feeling occurs among children as among adults. That is, children may not bring the same complexity of motive or scope of understanding to their emotional states as do adults. Thus it could be due to the lack of experience that children have had, as well as their state of intellectual development. We do know that young children have a short attention span, which could result in their capacity and propensity to change rapidly from one kind of emotion to another. As we mature into adulthood, rapid and irrational change in emotions is likely to decrease, or at least it should in normal adults. Nevertheless, we have seen a coach burst into a fit of anger when his team fumbles on the one-yard line, only to explode with joy when the team recovers an opponent's fumble on the next play. This exemplifies the strength of emotional influence of athletics events on otherwise rather calm individuals. It also illustrates the fact that emotions are sometimes subject to rapid change.

Emotions Can Appear with Various Degrees of Frequency

As individuals grow and mature, they manage to develop the ability to adjust to situations that previously would have caused an emotional reaction. This is no doubt due to the acquisition of more experience with various kinds of emotional situations. (This sometimes happens with coaches with long experience; they are described as more "mellow.") As far as children are concerned, they learn through experience what is socially acceptable and what is socially unacceptable. This is particularly true if a child is reprimanded in some way following a violent emotional reaction. As a result, a child may try to respond to a situation in ways that do not involve a strong emotional response. You probably know some adults who tend to react in much the same way.

People Differ in Their Emotional Responses

One person confronted with a situation that instills fear may run away from the immediate environment (hit-and-run driver), while another may try to hide from the cause of fear, or some may even laugh nervously or uncontrollably. The different reactions of people to emotional situations are probably due to a host of factors. Included among these may be past experience with a specific kind of emotional situation, willingness of parents and other adults during childhood to help them become more independent, and family relationships in general.

The Strength of People's Emotions Is Subject to Change

At some age levels certain kinds of emotions may be weak and at a later period become stronger. Conversely, with some children, emotions that were strong tend to decline. For example, young children may be timid among strangers, but later when they see there is nothing to fear, the timidity is likely to diminish. This may also be true of some adults who have experienced insecurity in childhood.

Emotional Arousals and Reactions

If we are to understand the nature of human emotions, we must understand the factors of emotional arousal and how people react to them. Many kinds of emotional patterns have been identified by researchers and discussed extensively. For our purposes, we have arbitrarily selected for discussion the emotional states of fear, worry, anger, jealousy, and joy.

Fear

The term fear, from the Old English *fir*, may have been derived originally from the German word *fahr*, meaning danger and peril. In modern times fear is often thought of in terms of anxiety caused by present or impending danger. For example, fear has often been defined as a more generalized reaction to a vague sense of threat in the absence of a specific or realistic dangerous object. However, the terms are often used loosely and almost interchangeably. When fearful or anxious, individuals experience unpleasant changes in overt behavior, subjective feelings (including thoughts), and physiological activity.

Fears differ from anxiety in that the former are negative emotional responses to any *specific* environmental factor. But fears and anxiety are similar in the feelings they arouse; rapid heartbeat, sweating, quivering, heavy breathing, feeling weak or numb in the limbs, dizziness or faintness, muscular tension, the need to eliminate, and a sense of dread—the fight or flight mechanism. Not all people experience all these signs of fear, but most experience some of them.

There are various ways of classifying fears. One way is to use the two broad classifications of *objective* and *irrational* fears. Many objective fears are useful and necessary, and it seems logical that we could be afraid of such things as touching a hot object, falling from a high place, and running into the street without looking for oncoming vehicles. These fears are said to be *rational* and *adaptive*.

Some fears are considered to be *irrational* and *maladaptive*. It is an irrational fear when the objective danger is disproportionate to the amount of distress experienced. These kinds of fears are called *phobias* or phobic disorders, some of which are: fear of high places, though one may be in no danger of falling; fear of closed-in, tight places when one is not necessarily in danger of being smothered or confined; fear of receiving injections—not because of the potential minor pain, but because of the "thought" of the procedure; fear of working with sharp instruments; fear of the dark; and fear of being alone.

Irrational fears or phobias do not necessarily have to interfere with our lives. It matters little if you are afraid of heights if your lifestyle permits you to avoid high places. However, other irrational fears can be debilitating experiences and interfere greatly with your attempt to lead your daily life. For instance, if you have no tolerance for the sight of blood or being in an environment of medical procedures, you may find your health or life endangered if you refrain from seeking treatment for an injury or disease. In these cases, it would clearly be of benefit to do something about such fears.

Individuals react differently to fears. In some the "ostrich" approach may be used. That is, people may hide their faces or cover their eyes to "get away from it." For example, some basketball coaches have been seen to "bury their face in their hands" when a player is about to attempt a crucial free throw. There is also the psychological phenomena of rationalizing away a threatening or troubling circumstance and the technique of simply convincing oneself to ignore the reality that typically would engender fear in the individual.

With the extraordinary emphasis on winning in college athletics, sometimes at almost any cost, it is not surprising that one of the greatest fears of coaches and athletic directors is the fear of losing. No wonder, because losing is often a threat to the budget, to morale, to image, and ultimately, to job security.

One of the fears of some college athletes is the fear of injury. In fact, some of them have professed that they "live in fear" of an injury that could be "career threatening" (especially in professional sports and for college athletes with a future career in professional sports). Other athletes play with "reckless abandon" and have little or no fear of suffering from injuries.

Worry

We have already mentioned that worry might be considered an imaginary form of fear. It can be a fear not aroused directly from one's environment or immediate circumstances. Worry can be aroused by imagining a situation that could *possibly* arise. That is, a coach could worry about whether or not he or she or an opponent will sign the prized recruit that both have been courting for some time. Since worries are likely to be caused by imaginary rather than real conditions, they are not likely to be found in abundance in very young children. Perhaps the reason for this is that young children have not reached a state of intellectual development where they might imagine certain things that could cause worry. Nor have they been profoundly impacted by troubling experiences at a level to engender substantial states of fearfulness. In many adults, worry is an acute and constant problem. This is most certainly true of many coaches and athletic directors as well. They often do not need to look far to find things about which to worry. Controlling worry is a compelling and constant problem for those adults who have difficulty in making needed adjustments in life situations.

Anger

One derivation of the word anger is from the Greek word *anchein,* which literally means a strong feeling of displeasure and usually antagonism. The emotional response of anger tends to occur more frequently than fear. This is probably due to the fact that there are more life conditions that incite anger. This has been illustrated in many coaching situations with some coaches frequently demonstrating moderate to intense anger toward players, assistants, and officials. Of course, the converse is true with some athletes, fans, and even sports writers who manifest anger toward coaches. Some children quickly learn that anger may get attention that otherwise would not be forthcoming. (Can you think of any childish adults who react in this manner?) It is likely that as children get older they may show more anger responses than fear responses because they soon see that there is not as much to fear as they originally thought. They also more frequently see anger-based behaviors modeled in their environments.

Because of individual differences, there is a wide variation in anger responses—and as mentioned previously, these responses are either impulsive or inhibited. It should be recalled that in impulsive responses, one manifests an overt action against another person or an object, such as kicking a door. This form of childish behavior is also sometimes manifested by adults.

Jealousy

Jealousy usually occurs when one feels a threat of the loss of affection or status. Many psychologists believe that jealousy is closely related to anger. Similar to anger, jealousy can build toward another person over time and become debilitating and dangerous if it develops into a prolonged, intense, and chronic state.

The individual responds in various ways. These responses might include: being aggressive toward the one he or she is jealous of, or possibly others as well; withdrawing from the person whose affections he or she thinks have been lost; and development of an "I don't care" attitude, but does not include withdrawal.

In some cases, individuals will not respond in any of these ways. They might try to excel over the person of whom they are jealous.

In other words, they might tend to do things to impress the person whose affections they thought had been lost or to regain the perceived loss of standing.

Joy

We strive for joy because this pleasant emotion is so important in maintaining emotional stability. Causes of joy differ from one age level to another, and from one person to another at the same age level. That is, a joyful situation for one person might not necessarily be joyful for another.

Joy is expressed in various ways, but the most common are laughing and smiling. Some people respond to joy with a state of body relaxation. This is difficult to detect because it has little or no overt manifestation. However, it may be perceptible when one compares it with body tension caused by unpleasant emotions. We have observed the coach who "heaves a sigh of relief" when the game finally ends, especially a highly competitive and close game.

Factors That Influence Emotionality

A person is considered emotionally fit when his or her emotions are properly controlled and when he or she is becoming more emotionally stable. This seems to indicate that emotional fitness is dependent to a certain extent upon known factors that influence emotionality. The following is a descriptive list of some of the factors that influence our emotions.

Fatigue

Fatigue tends to predispose people to irritability. We have seen this in the case of football or basketball coaches who begin to experience intense or prolonged fatigue during the course of their seasons. This is an expected and rather natural response to the fatigue and unrelenting pressure that they experience. Coaches, athletic directors, and student-athletes must find ways to manage their schedules in a way that fatigue does not result in negative, counterproductive, or embarrassing behaviors. Fatigue affects concentration and volatility. For this reason, it has been proven important to take a relaxation or food break during a busy and fatigue-intense day. In fact, some studies have shown that the hungrier a person is the more prone he or she is to outbursts of anger.

Inferior Health Status

Similar outcomes result when a person is in less than optimum health. Temporary poor health, such as colds, tend to make people irritable and reactive. Also, long-term health problems will often result in a more emotive state. Indeed, observations by the authors have shown that there are fewer emotional outbursts among healthy individuals than unhealthy individuals.

Intelligence

Studies tend to show that, on the average, persons with low intelligence have less emotional control than those with higher intelligence. This is probably due to the fact that there may be less frustration when a person is intelligent enough to understand the full meaning of his or her circumstances and to form perceptive conclusions regarding possible solutions. The reverse could also be true because people with high levels of intelligence are better able to perceive and identify things that would be likely to arouse emotions.

Social Environment

In a social environment where quarreling and unrest exist, a person is predisposed to unpleasant emotional conditions and more emotive reactions. Schedules that are too crowded and overly taxing can cause undue emotional excitation. The authors have frequently observed these conditions among coaches and athletes.

Aspiration Levels

If expectations are set beyond one's ability then emotionally unstable situations can occur. If a coach is not aware of athletes' limitations, he or she may set goals too high, and as a result, have too many failures. This can engender a more intense emotive state in the affected individuals and in the group.

All of the previously mentioned factors have been proved to have the potential for negative influence on emotions. Therefore, efforts would be made by a coach to understand and, where possible, eliminate these factors. Those that cannot be completely eliminated should be modified and kept under control.

EMOTIONAL REACTIVITY OF COACHES UNDER THE STRESS OF COMPETITION

The condition of competitive stress is pervasive in athletics. It occurs when coaches feel (perceive) that they will not be able to respond adequately to the performance demands of competition. When coaches feel this way, they experience considerable threat to self-esteem, resulting in stress. Also, competitive stress is a negative emotion that coaches experience when they perceive the competition to be personally threatening, such as a threat to their standing or continued employment in their present position.

Under the stress of competition coaches react with measurable emotional responses in the areas of blood pressure, blood sugar analysis, galvanic skin response, and heart rate.

Starting in the early 1950s, the late Warren Johnson, a former Professor of Health Education at the University of Maryland, was among the early pioneers who attempted to measure emotional reactivity in athletics. He used all of the previously discussed means of evaluating emotional reactivity and found all of them to have various limited degrees of validity. Although heart rate is slightly less valid than the others it is perhaps one of the most achievable means of assessing emotional reactivity of coaches during competitive events. The reason for this is that heart rate can be more easily monitored through the process of telemetry. Over a period of several years a number of studies have used this technique and examples of some of them are reported here.

In one study Gazes, Sovell, and Dellastatious[1] telemetered the heart rates of thirty basketball and football coaches from five minutes before until five minutes after a game, with the exception of halftime. Three coaches had pregame heart rates of less than 100 beats per minute. After a game started, each coach quickly reached a rate that was sustained, with minor changes, throughout the game. The maximum rate observed was 188 beats per minute in a coach who averaged 166 beats per minute throughout a game. His average rate during the game was 63 beats per minute above his resting heart rate.

Husman, Hanson, and Walker[2] monitored the heart rate of one varsity basketball coach. Under office conditions the coach's resting heart rate was 83 beats per minute. During a game that was publicized as being highly competitive, his average heart rate moved to 113 beats per minute for the first eight minutes of the second half. From then until the end of the game his heart rate averaged 135 beats per minute, and it was as high as 150 beats per minute during a free throw by the opposing team.

Porter and Allsen[3] measured the degree of increase in coaches' heart rates and compared the differences in the heart rates of the head and assistant basketball coaches. The subjects in this study were nine sets of head and assistant basketball coaches with team classifications ranging from high school junior varsity to NCAA Division I.

Each coach was pretested for maximum and resting heart rates. The maximum heart rate was measured while the subject ran on a standard-model treadmill until he or she was exhausted. In cases where physical restrictions prevented the use of the treadmill, the heart rates were measured on an electrocardiogram taken during thirty minutes' rest in a supine position.

Two biotelemetry systems that included surface electrodes, a transmitter, a receiver, and a tape recorder were used to measure the heart rates.

Each set of coaches was monitored for two games to gain a more accurate indication of the stress. The coaches were monitored continuously from ten minutes before until ten minutes after the games. No monitoring was done during halftime.

The highest average heart rate for a head coach during a game was 135 beats per minute, while the highest average rate for an assistant coach was 116 beats per minute.

The highest percentage above the resting heart rate for a head coach for a game was 126 percent, while the assistant coaches' heart rates reached a high of 82 percent above the resting heart rate.

The highest stress heart rate for a head coach over an extended period (more than ten consecutive minutes) was 158 beats per minute. This was 147 percent above his resting heart rate and 91 percent of his maximum heart rate. The highest stress heart rate for an assistant coach for an extended period was 139 beats per minute. This was 117 percent above his resting heart rate and 78 percent of his maximum heart rate.

The highest individual stress heart rate for a head coach was 162 beats per minute. This was 153 percent above his resting heart rate and 93 percent of his maximum heart rate. The highest individual stress heart rate for an assistant coach was 139 beats per minute (the same rate as for an extended period). This was 117 percent above his resting heart rate and 78 percent of his maximum heart rate.

As the games progressed, the stress became more intense until the games were over or until they were over in the judgment of the monitored subjects. Once the coaches (particularly the head coaches) has conceded to themselves either a victory or defeat due to a large point spread, the stress of responsibility seemed to be lifted and their heart rates decreased.

It was speculated that the difference between the stress on a head coach's heart compared to the stress on an assistant coach's heart is that an assistant coach makes suggestions while a head coach makes decisions. And of course the head coach would be held largely accountable for the results of those decisions. The investigators concluded that the emotional stress in basketball games as indicated by heart rates suggests that coaches should have an annual checkup of their cardiovascular system to determine any possible pathological problems, and further that coaches should also participate in regular cardiovascular exercise programs as a preventive measure.

McCafferty, Gliner, and Horvath[4] conducted a series of investigations to test the hypothesis that there may be similar stress on coaches of what might be referred to as nonrevenue sports as well as revenue sports. Coaches' heart rates were monitored during the last fifteen seconds of every minute throughout selected competitions by a telemetry apparatus.

Cross-country, which takes the competitors out of the sight of the coach, is an example of a sport that is likely to impose less stress. For example, the coach's heart rate while the runners were not in sight was only 79 beats per minute. However, an increase to 100 beats per minute was recorded while the runners were in view. Although this particular case showed little stress on the coach, another coach might have reacted differently.

The effect of the importance of a contest is illustrated by the heart rate response of a water polo coach to two games, one a preseason alumni game and the other a conference game. The coach's mean heart rates were not above 90 beats per minute for the alumni game, but during the conference game the mean rates were above 108 beats per minute. A standing heart rate of 144 beats per minute was also reported. The highest heart rate was observed during a time-out after four quick scores by the opponent. A few minutes later, when his team scored, the coach's heart rate dropped to 86 beats per minute. The stress of the alumni game was considerably less, but the coach's heart rate increased during the overtime period, again indicating that stress depends on situations that occur during the game. During the two games, the coach's mean heart rates were 37 (alumni game) and 55 (conference game) beats per minute higher than his normal standing heart rates. It appeared obvious from the heart rate response that the amount of stress on the coach varied considerably and that it depended on the perceived importance of the particular contest. In addition, there appeared to be a considerable amount of oscillation in the heart rate response precipitated by events during the contest.

This oscillation of heart rate response was also evident in a swimming coach during a swimming meet. Fluctuations of 30 to 50 beats per minute were observed repeatedly as the meet progressed. The fact that the coach's rate increased during each race demonstrated that the amount of stress depended on the particular event to which he was exposed.

These researchers concluded that the source of stress is the coach's perception of the events of the game and the meaning of the outcome, not necessarily the competitive requirements of the game itself. It was also concluded that profound alterations in a single stress indicator, heart rate, suggest the need for additional studies on the coach, and that the potential cardiovascular damage resulting from the behavioral and physiologic responses to stress should also be investigated. Two questions were raised: Does the coach require higher levels of cardiovascular fitness to diminish the possible harmful effects of the heart's response to stress? Would any activity after competition, such as relaxation or exercise, be beneficial?

Clearly, such questions should be investigated further since it is a well-documented fact that emotional upset caused by such factors as anger and fear that are stored up over time, can be a dangerous threat to a coach's health.

"The task of building and shaping a highly competitive or championship athletic team carries with it the built-in stress which intense competition naturally encompasses. The emotional reactivity of coaches reflects the compelling interplay between that stress and these emotion-based responses. The stress common in highly competitive coaching situations has been found to be similar in its effect/response to a soldier in battle, a race car driver in the pressure of a race and similarly highly stressful human activities."[5]

OPPORTUNITIES FOR THE DEVELOPMENT OF EMOTIONAL STABILITY IN THE ATHLETICS ENVIRONMENT

An athletics environment has the potential to develop a culture and environment that fosters emotional stability among its members. The extent to which this actually occurs is dependent primarily upon the kind of emotional climate desired by individuals responsible for it, such as coaches and athletic directors. Student-athletes will most often follow the lead of the directing adults in their athletics experience. For this reason, it appears pertinent to examine some of the opportunities that exist for the development of emotional stability in this environment. The following descriptive list is included for this purpose:

1. *Release of aggression in a socially acceptable manner.* This appears to be a highly functional way in which athletic activities can help provide opportunities to improve upon emotional stability. For example, kicking or hitting a ball, engaging in an aggressive penetration dribble, and many other athletic/com-

petitive maneuvers can afford a socially acceptable way of releasing aggression.

2. *Inhibition of direct response to unpleasant emotions.* This does not mean that all feelings concerned with such unpleasant emotions as fear and anger should be completely restrained. On the contrary, such feelings will sometimes take place less frequently and will be more effectively managed in a wholesome athletics environment (where emotional stability is perceived to be a primary value).

3. *Promotion of pleasant emotions.* Perhaps too much concern is placed upon suppressing unpleasant emotions and not enough attention given to promotion of pleasant ones. This means that the athletics experience should provide situations where a larger percentage of athletes can succeed at some level. This would mean that most of the athletes will have the opportunity for success at least some of the time.

4. *Understanding the ability and achievement of others.* In the athletics experience, emphasis can be placed upon achievements of the group, along with the function of each individual in the group. Team play, group effort, and group importance are integral in this matter.

5. *Being able to make a mistake without being depreciated or ostracized.* In the athletics setting, this requires that the coach serve as a catalyst who helps athletes understand the important concept of trial and error. Emphasis can be placed on trying and that one can learn not only from his or her own mistakes, but from the mistakes of others as well (the athletics field is not the "real world," but can be valuable preparation for it).

EVALUATING INFLUENCES OF THE ENVIRONMENT ON THE DEVELOPMENT OF EMOTIONAL STABILITY

We now move to the question of how the athletics environment contributes to emotional stability. To explore this question means that we will assess the environment itself with reference to whether or not these experiences are providing for emotional stability.

One such approach would be to refer back to the list of "opportunities for the development of emotional stability in the athletics environment" in the preceding discussion. These opportunities have been converted into a rating scale as follows:

1. The environmental experience provides for release of aggression in a socially acceptable manner.

   4 Most of the time
   3 Some of the time
   2 Occasionally
   1 Infrequently

2. The environmental experience provides for inhibition of direct response of unpleasant emotions.

   4 Most of the time
   3 Some of the time
   2 Occasionally
   1 Infrequently

3. The environmental experience provides for promotion of pleasant emotions.

   4 Most of the time
   3 Some of the time
   2 Occasionally
   1 Infrequently

4. The environmental experience provides for an understanding of the ability and achievement of others.

   4 Most of the time
   3 Some of the time
   2 Occasionally
   1 Infrequently

5. The environmental experience provides for being able to make a mistake without being depreciated or ostracized.

   4 Most of the time
   3 Some of the time
   2 Occasionally
   1 Infrequently

If one develops these ratings objectively and carefully, a reasonably good procedure for evaluation will result. Ratings can be made periodically to see if positive changes appear to be taking place. Ratings can be made for a single experience, a group of experiences, or for the total environmental experience. This procedure can help to identify the extent to which environmental experiences and/ or conditions under which the experiences take place are contributing to emotional stability.

EMOTIONALLY HEALTHY PERSONS

It seems appropriate to close this chapter by mentioning some of the characteristics of emotionally healthy persons. As we look at some of these characteristics we must recognize that they are not absolute nor are they static. We are not always happy and we sometimes find ourselves in situations in which we are not adequately confident. In fact, sometimes we may feel inadequate to solve commonplace problems that occur in our work and personal lives. But we should continuously attempt to develop those traits that characterize an emotionally healthy person. These characteristics are indeed important for those involved in athletics:

1. Emotionally healthy persons have achieved basic harmony within themselves and a workable relationship with others. They are able to function effectively, and with some level of contentment, even though they are keenly aware of the challenges and limitations involved in the human experience.
2. Emotionally healthy persons manage to adapt to the demands of environmental conditions with emotional responses that are appropriate in degree and kind to the stimuli and situations— with responses that fall, generally, within the range of what is considered "normal" in society.
3. Emotionally healthy persons face problems directly and seek realistic and plausible solutions to them. They try to free themselves from excessive and unreal anxieties, worries and fears—even though they are aware that there is often much to be concerned about professionally and personally in our complex society.

4. Emotionally healthy persons have developed a guiding philosophy of life and have a set of core values. The values are internalized, acceptable to themselves, and are generally in harmony with the values of society that are reasonable and conducive to individual integrity and the common good.

5. Emotionally healthy persons accept and affirm themselves and are able to deal with the world as it exists in reality. They accept what cannot be changed at a particular time and place. They derive satisfaction within the framework of their own strengths and those of their environment.

6. Emotionally healthy persons tend to be well-adjusted and reasonably happy. They tend to have an enthusiasm for living. While they are aware of their limitations, they do not focus their attention upon their inadequacies and weaknesses. They view those around them with the same balance and positive realism.

7. Emotionally healthy persons have a variety of satisfying interests and they maintain a balance between their work, personal responsibilities, and recreation. They find constructive and satisfying outlets for creative expression in the interests that they pursue.

This list of characteristics of emotionally healthy persons presents a near-ideal situation and obviously none of us function at these high levels at all times. However, they might well be considered as suitable guidelines and worthy goals for which we can strive. The balanced pursuit of these will help an individual deal with, and possibly prevent, some of the unpleasant emotional stress that naturally accompanies participation as an athlete or professional in an athletics environment—as well as in life in general.

It is exceedingly important that coaches, athletes, and athletic administrators understand the nature, scope, and power of emotions in their environment. The emotion and the passion that characterize much of the total athletics experience are factors that have profound impact on all those involved in athletics and extends their impact to fans, alumni, and the collegiate community.[6]

Chapter 6

A Healthful
Stress-Management Lifestyle

At the outset of this chapter we want to recall the extent to which athletes, coaches, and athletic directors practiced the following principle of living: *Personal health practices should be carefully observed.* Sixty percent of the athletes, 56 percent of the coaches, and about 35 percent of the athletic directors reported that they practiced this beneficial principle.

Many of the respondents indicated only partial or modest success with this principle of living. Particularly among coaches, a number admitted to neglecting sleep and rest with sixteen- to twenty-hour work days. Others said that they sometimes watched game films "well into the night" to try to gain an advantage on the opponent (while perhaps putting themselves at a disadvantage through loss of sleep). Others felt that their eating habits during the season could be improved.

The goal of stress management is to improve one's lifestyle. The purpose of this chapter, therefore, is to provide sound information about a lifestyle that will result in a better personal stress-management system for athletes, coaches, and athletic directors—and how this can be achieved in part by practicing good health habits.

Basic to the control and reduction of stress is the attention people pay to their own personal health. There are two general factors to consider with regard to stress and health. First, objective evidence continues to accumulate to support the idea that prolonged stressful conditions can be detrimental to the health of many individuals. Second, along with modern techniques of reducing stress are many traditional health practices that long have enabled people to gain greater control over anxieties and help relieve the effects of stressful living. In this chapter we will discuss the second factor in the anticipation that the discussion will also help eliminate, or at least minimize, the first factor.

In discussing the subject of caring for one's health, we will deal with what we will call the "Health and Fitness Triangle": (1) nutrition and diet, (2) body restoration, and (3) physical activity and exercise. Before getting into specific discussions of these three areas, it will be helpful to discuss the general area of health.

THE MEANING OF HEALTH

The exact meaning that we associate with the term health depends in a large measure upon the particular frame of reference in which the word is used. In past years it was a common practice to think of health in terms of the condition of a living body that is functioning normally. This concept of health is still accepted by many people—including many in our surveys of athletes, coaches, and athletic directors. In subscribing to this particular concept some individuals tend to think of health predominantly as a state in which pain or symptoms are absent related to a poorly functioning organism. When thought of only in this manner, *health is concerned primarily in terms of a state in which there is absence of disease.*

In modern times health is being considered more and more in terms of *well-being,* which is perhaps our most important human condition. In considering health from the viewpoint of well-being, the ideal state of health would perhaps be one in which all of the various parts of the human body function at an optimum level at all times. Although it is very unlikely that the human body will ever achieve this ideal state, such a level is ordinarily used as a standard for diagnosing or appraising the human health status.

The old meaning that considered health primarily in terms of absence of disease tended to place health in a *negative* sense. The modern concept places more *positive* emphasis on the term. Thus, health is now correctly interpreted as a level of well-being also. It seems logical to assume that modern society's goal should be directed toward achieving the highest level of well-being for all of its citizens.

Health Knowledge, Attitudes, and Practices

Any discussion of human health should consider these three important aspects: health knowledge, attitudes, and practices. Each of these dimensions will be dealt with separately in the ensuing discussion. But it appears important first to consider them together for the purposes of a better understanding of how they are interdependent and interrelated in regard to human health.

In order to benefit from health learning experiences, it is most important that these experiences develop into desirable, consistent health practices. Thus, the ultimate goal should be in the development of a kind of behavior that is likely to ensure optimum present and future health for the individual. However, before the most desirable and worthwhile health practices can be achieved, there is a need for a certain amount of desirable health knowledge along with a proper attitude in applying this knowledge to health practices.

It is obvious that *to know* is not necessarily *to do*. Nevertheless, that which is done wisely will depend in a large measure upon the kind and amount of knowledge one has acquired. In the accumulation of health knowledge one will need to understand *why* it is beneficial to follow a certain practice. When one knows why, it is more likely that he or she will develop a more positive attitude toward beneficial health practices. When a person acquires desirable health knowledge by learning valid health concepts (and also has a proper health attitude) then he or she will more likely apply the knowledge in health behavior. Furthermore, one should be in a better position to exercise good judgment and make wise decisions in matters pertaining to health if the right kind and amount of health knowledge has been obtained.

Health Knowledge

Knowledge about health is acquired in a variety of ways. Some of it is the product of tradition, sometimes simply folklore. Many people still hold strongly to certain popular health-related notions long after those ideas have been dispelled by the scientific community. These individuals, for a variety of reasons, have not benefitted from modern health knowledge.

Other kinds of health knowledge are derived in our modern society from the constant bombardment of our culture by mass communications media such as television, print, and radio. Although some of this information may be valid from a health standpoint, everyone should be aware that the primary purpose of many kinds of advertising is to sell a product, and that sometimes the advertisements claim results that are not always attainable.

Another source of health knowledge is the home. In fact, much of our important health knowledge originates in the home. Parents are our first teachers. What we learn from them, often without our being aware that we are learning it, tends to remain with us. A beneficial home setting should contribute much to the health knowledge of its children simply by providing good meals as well as a friendly, well-regulated, pleasant, and recreationally challenging environment in which to develop and grow. Children from such homes ordinarily do not have to unlearn a lot of faulty ideas and unwholesome attitudes when they arrive at the next great potential source of health knowledge—the schools. It should be kept in mind that many children who grow up in homes in the inner city and some remote parts of the country do not benefit from good home health experiences and thus their first source of beneficial knowledge is the school.

The scope of knowledge that one might obtain about matters related to health is almost endless. Obviously it would be almost impossible to learn everything about human health. However, certain basic concepts about health should be developed by individuals at all age levels. Generally speaking, the individual should acquire knowledge pertaining to the basic needs of the body—plus knowledge regarding the human body as it functions in its environment. It is important to remember that education is a lifelong process and all of us should attempt to obtain the best health information available from valid sources throughout our lifetime. Information regarding human health is constantly changing. The enormous, continuing research activities regarding health provide us with new information almost daily.

Health Attitudes

Any discussion of attitudes requires an identification of the meaning of the term. It is recognized that different meanings are attached to the term attitude. But for our purposes, this term will be thought of as associated with *feelings*. We hear such expressions as "How do you *feel* about it?" In a sense, this implies, "What is your *attitude* toward it?" Therefore, attitude can be considered a factor in the instigation and nature of action. For example, knowledge alone that exercise is beneficial will not necessarily lead to regular exercising, but the presence of a positive feeling or attitude would be a determining factor that leads one to exercise regularly.

A disclaimer should be noted here, however. Limited objective evidence exists to support unequivocally the notion that attitude has a universally positive, direct influence on behavior. One of the difficulties in studying this phenomenon scientifically lies in the questionable validity of instruments used to measure attitude. In addition, no wide agreement is evident with regard to the meaning of attitudes. Thus, the position taken here is one of theoretical postulation based upon logical assumption.

Health attitudes might be viewed as a gap that can exist between health knowledge and health practice. This gap needs to be bridged if effective health behavior is to result from acquiring valid health knowledge. Consider as an example a person who has acquired knowledge regarding the degree to which cigarette smoking can be harmful to health. Perhaps the person will have some kind of underlying feeling or attitude toward such knowledge. He or she may choose to disregard it because some friends have also assumed such an attitude toward it. Or the person may feel that the evidence is convincing enough, and believe that he or she can or should stop smoking. In either case, the person has developed an attitude toward the practice of cigarette smoking and may act in accordance with this feeling. It should also be mentioned that the person may not react in accordance with his or her true feelings because he or she considers it fashionable to smoke cigarettes or may elect not to proceed through the rigors and trauma of cessation. The individual's chosen response will be tempered at least to an extent by the consequences that are associated with the knowledge acquired about cigarette smoking.

Obviously, one would hope that the accumulation of health knowledge would be accompanied by a positive attitude, and that this attitude would result in desirable action. It is probable that only when a positive attitude is present regarding good health practices, will the individual meaningfully pursue such health practices. Attitude is integral and, indeed, the catalyst.

Health Practices

It was suggested previously that *to know* is not necessarily *to do*. Clearly, all people do not use meaningfully the knowledge that they have acquired. Many act primarily only on impulse. Others are influenced largely by the actions of their friends or peer group. However, in a matter as important as one's health, it appears reasonable to follow a course in which the individual weighs the facts and scientific evidence and then charts a beneficial course of action.

One might look at beneficial as well as undesirable health practices. If one weighs knowledge in these terms, then perhaps one can better appreciate the possible consequences of individual health practices.

To change behavior is sometimes quite difficult. However, it is hoped that most individuals will want to make a positive modification of their own health behavior after acquiring health knowledge and forming favorable attitudes. In the final analysis, the individual will make the decisions regarding his or her own health practices.

In business settings it is often said that "profit is born of risk." In contemporary society the reverse might be true in terms of the risks that people tend to take in matters pertaining to their health. Personal health becomes a matter of how much risk one is willing to take. One's health practices are often based on this factor. To illustrate this we will refer again to cigarette smoking and health. It has never been demonstrated scientifically that cigarette smoking is in any way beneficial to the physical health of the human body. On the contrary, a great deal of validated medical information indicates that smoking can contribute to a number of serious diseases. Yet millions of people, including some college athletes, are willing to assume a dangerous risk in defiance of such evidence.

After learning about some aspect of health, the individual is left with the element of choice. We hope to see a course of health action chosen that will involve a minimum of health risk.

A LIFESTYLE THAT ENCOMPASSES
THE HEALTH AND FITNESS TRIANGLE

Three basic essentials are needed to maintain the human organism at a reasonable level of health. These are (a) intake and utilization of proper foods, (b) adequate body restoration, and (c) sufficient exercise. We have already labeled this triad the *Health and Fitness Triangle* and the following discussions will focus on how these health factors can assist one in keeping undesirable stress under control.

Nutrition

Nutrition can be described as the sum of the processes by which a person takes in and utilizes food substances; that is, the nourishment of the body by food. These processes consist of ingestion, digestion, absorption, and assimilation.

Ingestion derives from the Latin word "ingestus" meaning to take in and here it means taking in food, or the act of eating. The process of *digestion* involves the breaking down and conversion of food into substances that can be *absorbed* through the lining of the intestinal tract and into the blood and used by the body. *Assimilation* is concerned with the incorporation or conversion of nutrients into *protoplasm,* which is the essential material making up the living cells.

The body needs many essential nutrients or foods to keep it functioning properly. These nutrients fall into the broad groups of proteins, carbohydrates, fats, minerals, and vitamins (although water is not a nutrient in the strictest sense of the word, it must be included, for nutrition cannot take place without it).

Three major functions of nutrients are building and repair of all body tissues, regulation of all body functions, and providing fuel for the body's energy needs. Although all the nutrients can do their best work when they are in combination with other nutrients, each still has its own vital role to play.

Diet

Diet is an all-inclusive term used to refer to foods and liquids regularly consumed. The question is often raised, "What constitutes a balanced diet?" Essentially, one answer is that along with sufficient fluids, one should include foods from the four basic food groups: dairy, meat, vegetables and fruits, and breads and cereals.

A guide to a balanced diet was prepared in 1997 by the staff of the United States Senate Select Committee on Nutrition and Human Needs. This committee spent a great deal of time with hearings and research. Some of its recommendations are listed as follows.

1. Eat less meat and more fish and poultry.
2. Replace whole milk with skim milk.
3. Reduce intake of eggs, butter, and other high cholesterol foods.
4. Cut back on sugars to 15 percent of daily caloric intake.
5. Reduce intake of salt to a total of three grams per day.
6. Eat more fruit, vegetables, and whole grains.

Note: Any radical departure from one's diet should be made only under the guidance of a physician and/or a qualified nutritionist.

The above recommendations are directed to the general population. However, it is important to remember that eating is an individual matter. The problem may not be so much one of following an arbitrary diet. Rather, it is learning which foods and what proportions of foods keep the individual functioning best. The body is capable of compensating for an imbalance in the nutrients that the person intakes if the shortage is made up within a reasonable period of time. In other words, it is not necessary to have an exactly balanced diet at every meal. Indeed, it is possible to miss meals or even go several days without food—and show no signs of malnutrition (of course, we are not recommending that you do this). The important consideration seems to be in the quality of the total intake over a period of time.

The foregoing observations should not be interpreted to mean that one should be indifferent or careless about food choices. The seventeenth-century gastronomist, Anthelme Brillat-Savarin, famous for his book *The Physiology of Taste*, once said, "Tell me what you eat and I will tell you what you are." The more modern adage, "You are what you eat" could well have been derived from this old quotation.

It is absurd that some people are more careful about what they feed their pets than they are about what they feed themselves. This kind of carelessness has given rise to the claim that Americans are at once the most overfed and yet among the most malnourished people in the world.

The adage, "You are what you eat," has been brought more clearly into focus because researchers now know that our bodies synthesize food substances that become *neurotransmitters*. Prominent nutritionists tend to believe that these neurotransmitters relay messages to the brain which, in turn, affect our moods, sex drive, appetite, and even personality. This is to say that adding a certain food or omitting another could be just what a person might need for healthful living. It is believed that when a person is stressed the body becomes less able to make use of protein. Therefore, the general recommendation is that after any kind of profound stress is experienced one should eat more lean meat, fish, or milk products. Also, since stress depletes the supply of vitamin C and potassium, these should be replaced by adding to the diet extra portions of citrus products.

The diets of some families include too much of certain foods that can be potentially harmful. A case in point is the intake of cholesterol. Excessive amounts of this chemical component of animal oils and fats are deposited in the blood vessels and may be a factor in hardening of the arteries, leading to a heart attack.

The universal interest in this risk factor is certainly justified by such estimates as:

1. Over 50 percent of Americans have a cholesterol level that is too high.
2. Only about 8 percent of Americans know their cholesterol level.
3. As many as 250,000 lives could be saved each year if citizens were tested and took action to reduce their cholesterol.
4. For every 1 percent cholesterol is lowered, you reduce your risk of heart attack by 2 percent.
5. If your cholesterol is 265 or over, you have four times the risk of heart attack as someone with 190 or less.

6. Nine out of ten people can substantially reduce their cholesterol level by a combination of diet and exercise. In fact, people with high cholesterol need to exercise to get the full benefit of a healthy diet.

It should be mentioned that not all cholesterol is bad. The two kinds of lipoproteins are low-density lipoproteins (LDL) and high-density lipoproteins (HDL). The former is considered "bad" because the cholesterol it carries is associated with an increased risk of hardening of the inner lining of arteries. HDL (good) appears to clear excess cholesterol from the arteries, while LDL (bad) can lead to cholesterol buildup in the artery walls.

Physicians vary widely in their beliefs about safe levels of cholesterol. Not too long ago a broad range of 150 to 300 was considered normal. However, thoughts on this matter have changed radically. For example, the National Heart, Lung, and Blood Institute has announced more stringent guidelines. It is now believed that total blood cholesterol should not exceed 200 (meaning 200 milligrams of total cholesterol per deciliter of blood).

As far as stress and cholesterol are concerned, it has been demonstrated that stress has a much more powerful influence on serum lipids and cholesterol than dietary fat intake.[1] Stress-related hormones elevate serum lipids by breaking down fat stores in the body. Stress also contributes to accelerated atherosclerosis because it promotes free radical production. Free radicals are responsible for other manifestations of the aging process, such as wrinkled skin, grey hair, cataracts, and cancer, which helps to explain the close link between stress and premature aging.

Diet and Weight Control

Basically, weight gain or loss is a matter of energy intake versus energy expenditure of the body. If one wishes to decrease body fat one can reduce caloric intake (which is most easily done by reducing the amount of high-energy foods) and increase energy expenditure (by means of physical activity). By doing both, one can lower the weight a given amount in a given time by less severe dieting than would otherwise be necessary to accomplish the same thing. Some authorities feel that it may be a mistake to make reducing a matter of "willpower." As in trying to stop smoking, willpower may set up a desperate struggle from which the habit is likely to emerge victorious. Or a substitute habit may be acquired, as in the case of the man who gave up drinking altogether—and since has become a helplessly obsessive gambler. The wise course might be to determine *why* eating has become disproportionately important in life and, as in the case cited earlier, discover what needs to be done about it.

Dieting is the most popular way of controlling weight. Therefore, it seems appropriate to establish general principles when one undertakes the regimen. The following list of principles might well be considered by anyone contemplating a weight control program:

1. Seek the advice of a physician and/or qualified nutritionist.
2. If fat is to be lost, the calories taken in must be fewer than those needed for the body's energy requirements.
3. The diet, though low in calories, must be adequate in all other nutrients so that intakes of these do not become dangerously low.
4. It should be recognized that losing weight is not easy.
5. Foods are not forbidden, but portion control is emphasized.
6. A sensible balance of energy-producing nutrients should be present.
7. The diet should be realistic and should not call for superhuman effort.
8. Exercise concurrent with modified food intake at the same time is recommended.
9. The behaviors and emotions that lead to excessive eating should be examined. Advice should be sought to help the dieter control these.

Diet and Stress

With few exceptions, writers on the subject of stress emphasize the importance of diet as a general health measure. However, the question that should be asked is: "Are there any specific forms of diet that can contribute to the prevention of stress and/or help one cope with stress?" (We have already mentioned how some foods might be used when one is under stress, and later we will comment on the controversy surrounding the use of the so-called "stress formula vitamins.")

According to one authority on the subject of food and stress management, Paul J. Rosch, President of the American Institute of Stress,[2] no universal diet has been proven to relieve stress. However, there are some general recommendations that can help one stay healthy and also lower the risk for developing cardiovascular diseases and certain cancers. These would most certainly apply to individuals involved in athletics and under the stressors discussed earlier. Some of these recommendations include:

1. Try to eat a variety of foods in amounts designed to achieve a healthy weight.
2. Vegetables, fruits, grain products, and complex carbohydrates are most likely to help you reach and maintain this goal.
3. Limit your intake of refined sugar, salt, and alcohol.
4. Avoid foods high in sodium, saturated fats, and cholesterol content.
5. Try to drink eight glasses of water per day.
6. Make sure that you have an adequate intake of essential nutrients and vitamins, especially if you are trying to lose weight.

The last two items are particularly important with respect to stress. Water is an important element that is often neglected in planning a diet. If one is under stress or perspiring because of exercise or the heat, then one naturally needs to drink even more water. Coffee and cola drinks are not good substitutes, since they contain caffeine, which acts as a diuretic. All chemical reactions that transform food into energy in the body require water. The brain is about 75 percent water by weight, and is the first organ to be affected by dehydration. Although symptoms may not occur unless fluid depletion is severe, deficiencies do keep one from thinking and performing at an optimum level—and could produce or aggravate stress-related complaints such as fatigue and headache. To avoid this, one needs sufficient water each day to replace lost fluids. It is best not to try to accomplish this all at once, or to drink only when you are thirsty. Juice, milk, and caffeine-free sodas are acceptable alternatives, although they should not replace needed water intake entirely. It should be mentioned, however, that overindulgence in some of the so-called sports drinks could cause deterioration of tooth enamel.

Vitamins and Stress

From a historical point of view, the realization that vitamins are basic nutrients stands as a milestone in the emergence of the field of nutrition science. Unlike such nutrients as protein, fats, and minerals, vitamins do not become a part of the structure of the body, but rather serve as catalysts that make possible various chemical reactions within the body. These reactions have to do with converting food substances into the elements needed for utilization by the various cells of the body. For example, vitamin D must be present if calcium is to be metabolized and made available for use in the blood and bones.

The vitamins with which we are familiar today are commonly classified as *fat*-soluble and *water*-soluble. This designation means that the one group requires fatty substances and the other water, if they are to be dissolved and used by the body. Although a large number of vitamins have been identified as being important to human nutrition, the exact function of some of them has not yet been determined.

In countries such as the United States it is not generally difficult for people to select a diet that is sufficiently varied to include all necessary vitamins. However, poor dietary practices can lead to vitamin inadequacy. As a precaution many people supplement their diets with vitamin pills and other forms of vitamin supplements. Even though such supplements may not be needed, when taken in small amounts the vitamins may do no harm. This is particularly true of the water-soluble vitamins because if one gets more than necessary, they will pass right through the body. (Recently, some scientists have been disputing this claim, especially if water-soluble vitamins are taken in extra large doses.) On the other hand, some of the fat-soluble vitamins may be toxic and overdoses could cause harm. Of course, extra vitamins may be prescribed by physicians for a variety of reasons ranging from suspected malnutrition, to chronic fatigue and postsurgical recovery.

In recent years a great deal of controversy has emerged as a result of what has been called *megavitamin therapy*, which is related to the use of certain vitamins in massive doses, sometimes as much as 1,000 times the U.S. Recommended Daily Allowances. The proponents for megavitamin therapy believe that massive doses of such vitamins (particularly vitamin C, vitamin E, and the B-complex vitamins) will prevent certain diseases and very significantly extend life. Opponents of the practice maintain that it not only may be useless, but in some instances harmful as well.

It is interesting to note that some support exists for massive doses of certain vitamins as an important factor in surviving stress. In fact, there is a special class of vitamins sold over the counter called *stress formula vitamins*. The formula for many of these includes large amounts of vitamin C and vitamin B-complex.

In this general regard, a recent report[3] is noteworthy. That is, there is no good evidence that these so-called stress formula vitamins will replenish nutrients lost during emotional stress or will actually reduce stress. In the 1950s the National Academy of Science issued a report suggesting that people might need more C and B vitamins during severe physical stress. That meant multiple injuries, severe burns, or major surgery, not the stress from going through a divorce or work-related stress.

Anyone contemplating a vitamin supplement over and above the U.S. Recommended Daily Allowances should do so in consultation with a physician or qualified nutritionist.

Nutritional and Dietary Disorders in Athletes

We have already reported in Chapter 3 that some athletes suffer digestive disorders because of stress. However, a much more serious nutritional and dietary disorder is anorexia nervosa. This is particularly evident in female athletes.

The condition of anorexia nervosa is characterized by an obsession with losing weight. The following criteria for this disorder have been determined by the American Psychiatric Association:[4]

1. Intense fear of becoming obese, which does not diminish as weight loss progresses
2. Disturbance in the way in which one's body weight, size, or shape is experienced (claiming to "feel fat" when the individu-

al is thin or even emaciated; belief that one area of the body is "too fat" even when obviously underweight)

3. Refusal to maintain body weight over a minimal normal weight for age and height (e.g., weight loss leading to maintenance of body weight 15 percent below expected; failure to make expected weight gain during period of growth, leading to body weight 15 percent below expected)

4. In females, absence of at least three consecutive menstrual cycles when otherwise expected to occur (primary or secondary amenorrhea)

This condition is about ten times more prevalent among females than males, because a higher percent of females are preoccupied with thinness.

Anorexics use all sorts of ways to lose weight, such as drastically reducing food intake and self-induced vomiting. This is a very serious condition and when it is identified it should be treated immediately.

The condition among some female college athletes, particularly in such sports as swimming, gymnastics, and track and field, is said to be due in part to the type of apparel used in participation; that is, the "skintight" uniform tends to display one's figure in detail. The perception of the athletes is that they want to be seen as lean and fit, especially when an athletics competition is viewed by a significant number of spectators.

Another condition known as bulimia nervosa, while not as prevalent among athletes, at the same time is extremely serious. Bulimia can best be described as binge eating, or rapid ingestion of large quantities of food over a short period of time. The American Psychiatric Association has established the following criteria for this disorder:[5]

1. Recurrent episodes of binge eating (rapid consumption of a large amount of food in a discrete period of time, usually less than two hours)

2. Fear of not being able to stop eating during eating binges

3. Regular occurrences of either self-induced vomiting, use of laxatives, or rigorous dieting or fasting to counteract the effects of the binge eating

4. A minimum average of two binge-eating episodes per week for at least three months

Again, this is an extremely serious condition and requires immediate medical attention.

Many college athletics departments maintain the services of conditioning coaches and sports nutritionists. A part of their responsibility is to monitor the eating habits of athletes. This can be of particular importance for female athletes because insufficient nutrition leading to anorexia can be the cause of missed menstrual periods that can lead to lower estrogen levels in the body. Also, athletes on acute or near-starvation diets may lose muscle mass and energy, which in turn can detract from their athletic performance and, more important, can damage the health of the individual.

Body Restoration

In order to be effective and to enjoy life, periodic recuperation is essential. Body restoration in the form of rest and sleep provides us with the necessary means of revitalizing ourselves—allowing us to meet our challenges and responsibilities. To keep fatigue at a minimum and in its proper proportion in the cycle of everyday activities, nature has provided us with ways to help combat and reduce fatigue.

It is important that individuals such as athletes, coaches, and athletic directors (who function under the physical and mental stressors previously discussed) understand the dynamics of human fatigue and body restoration.

There are two types of fatigue—*acute* and *chronic*. Acute fatigue is a natural outcome of sustained or severe exertion. It is due to such physical factors as the accumulation of the by-products of muscular exertion in the blood and to excessive "oxygen debt"—the inability of the body to take in as much oxygen as is being consumed by the muscular work. Psychological considerations may also be important in acute fatigue. That is, an individual who becomes bored with his or her situation, and who becomes preoccupied with the discomfort involved, will become fatigued much sooner than if he or she is highly motivated to do the same thing, is not bored, and does not think about the discomfort.

Chronic fatigue has reference to fatigue that lasts over extended periods—in contrast with acute fatigue, which tends to be followed by a recovery phase and restoration to normal within a more or less brief period of time. Chronic fatigue may be due to any one of a variety of medical conditions (such conditions are the concern of the physician, who should evaluate all cases of chronic fatigue to assure that a disease condition is not responsible). It may also be due to psychological factors such as extreme boredom and/or worry of having to do, over an extended period, what one does not wish to do.

Fatigue tends to predispose people to irritability. Consequently, we do things to modify fatigue such as "taking a break" at selected times during the day. This is an important factor that coaches need to consider during demanding practice sessions.

Rest

In general, most people think of rest as just "taking it easy." A chief purpose of rest is to reduce tension so that the body may be better able to recover from fatigue. No overt activity is involved, but neither is loss of consciousness experienced, as in sleep. Since the need for rest is usually in direct proportion to the type of activity in which we engage, it follows naturally that the more strenuous the activity, the more frequent the rest periods should be. A busy day on the job may not be as noticeably active nor as strenuous as a game of tennis. Nevertheless, a wise person will let the body dictate when a rest period is required. Five or ten minutes of sitting in a chair with the eyes closed may make a significantly positive difference in the course of an active day, assuming that this is possible. The real effectiveness of rest periods depends largely on the individual and his or her ability to slow the pace of activity, relax, and then rest. (Coaches who are under severe stress have reported that their attempts to relax or rest during the work day/evening are not usually successful because of the pervasive stress that they perceive themselves to experience for prolonged periods.)

Sleep

Sleep is a phenomenon that has never been clearly defined or understood, but which has aptly been named the "great restorer."

Authorities on the subject agree that sleep is essential to the vital functioning of the body and that natural sleep is the most satisfying form of recuperation from fatigue. Clearly, it is during the hours of sleep that the body is given an opportunity to revitalize itself. All vital functions are slowed so that the building of new cells and the repair of tissues can take place without undue interruption. This does not mean that the body builds and regenerates tissue only during sleep, but it does mean that it is the time that nature has set aside to accomplish the task more readily. The body's metabolic rate is lowered and energy is restored.

Despite the acknowledged need for sleep, a question of paramount importance concerns the amount of sleep necessary for the body to accomplish its recuperative task. There is no clear-cut answer to this query. Sleep is an individual matter, based on degree rather than kind. The usual recommendation for adults is eight hours of sleep out of every twenty-four, but the basis for this could well be one of fallacy rather than fact. There are many people who can function effectively on less sleep, while others require more. No matter how many hours of sleep you get during the course of a twenty-four-hour period, the best test of adequacy will depend largely on how you feel. If you are normally alert, feel healthy, and are in good humor, you are probably getting a sufficient amount of sleep. The recuperative effect that sleep normally brings to the body depends to a large extent upon a person's freedom from excessive emotional tension and ability to relax. Unrelaxed sleep has more limited restorative value, but learning to relax is a skill that is not easily acquired.

Is loss of sleep dangerous? This question is pondered quite frequently. Again, the answer is not simple. To the normally healthy person with normal sleep habits, occasionally missing the accustomed hours of sleep is not usually serious. On the other hand, repeated loss of sleep over a period of time can be dangerous. It is the loss of sleep night after night, rather than on isolated occasions, that apparently is the most damaging and results in the condition previously described as chronic fatigue.

The general effects of loss of sleep are likely to result in poor general health. But, in addition to damage to one's individual health, there is another aspect of what we will call the *cost of sleepiness.* One report[6] indicates that errors due to sleepiness cost the United States $56 billion per year. Thousands of deaths and millions of disabling injuries also result from accidents related to sleepiness. Surveys show that 20 percent of adults show up late for work or miss work entirely because of not sleeping well the previous night.

Many conditions tend to rob the body of restful slumber. Mental anguish and worry have been shown to have a significantly negative effect on sleep. Numerous coaches, athletes, and athletic directors report this condition during the course of their recruiting periods, competitive seasons, and budget planning periods. Other factors that influence the quality of sleep are hunger, cold, boredom, and excessive fatigue. However, in many instances these factors can be managed and kept under control.

Numerous recommendations about sleep have been made by various sources. Some of these recommendations are summarized below:

1. Relax physically and mentally before retiring for sleep.
2. Reduce tension level during the day.
3. Manage your time, activities, and thoughts to prepare for a restorative night's sleep.
4. The process should be the same each night, should begin at the same hour and should lead to repose at the same hour.
5. Avoid stimulants before retiring. Indeed, for some people a glass of warm milk or a warm shower have been found to promote sleep.

Understanding the complex nature of sleep may be the province of scientists and other qualified experts, but an understanding of the value of sleep is the responsibility of every person.

Physical Activity and Exercise

A good proportion of the athletes, coaches, and athletic directors in our surveys indicated that they engage in some sort of physical activity and exercise to combat stress. Activities most frequently identified were various forms of net games such as racquetball, badminton, and tennis; jogging; basketball; and weight training.

Although most coaches and athletic directors engaged in activities, many said it was done on a more or less sporadic basis. Many professed that they should be on some kind of regular exercise program, but are not.

When used in connection with the human organism, the term *physical* means a concern for the body and its needs. The term *activity* derives from the word *active,* one meaning of which is the *requirement of action.* Thus, when the two words physical and activity are used together, it implies body action. This is a broad term and could include any voluntary and/or involuntary body movement. When such body movement is practiced for the purpose of developing and maintaining physical fitness, it is ordinarily referred to as physical exercise.

Maintaining a Suitable Level of Physical Fitness

Physical fitness presupposes an adequate intake of food and an adequate amount of rest and sleep, but also includes activity involving all the large muscles of the body. When we ask, "Just *how high a level* of physical fitness should be maintained from one stage of life to another?" we raise another very important question: "Fitness for what?" Obviously, the young varsity athlete needs to think of a level of fitness far above that which will concern the average adult—including most coaches and athletic directors.

Physical fitness has been described in many ways. However, when all of these descriptions are assembled, it is likely that they will seem more similar than widely different. We should think of physical fitness as the level of ability of the human organism to perform certain physical tasks. Or put another way, it is the fitness to perform various specified tasks requiring muscular effort.

The word exercise may tend to have moralistic or imperative overtones. Like so many things that are said to be "good for you," it also tends to give rise to feelings of boredom and resentment. Thus, many people are pleased facetiously to recite such old sayings as: "When I feel like exercising, I lie down quickly until the feeling goes away," or "I get my exercise serving as pall-bearer for my friends who exercised."

Maintaining some level of physical fitness makes possible many kinds of meaningful experiences in life that are not otherwise available to the individual. These experiences include all manner of physical activity and exercise, including indoor and outdoor sports. They also include the rich and satisfying interpersonal relationships that are often associated with these activities.

Developing Your Own Program

Those involved in athletics usually have available to them the services and facilities for participation in regularly planned physical activities. They have a distinct advantage over those for whom such services are not provided. However, they may also be interested in some of the factors that are concerned with embarking on a program.

The traditional recommendation has been to consult a physician before undertaking a physical activity or physical fitness program. However, a recent publication[7] by the National Heart, Lung, and Blood Institute (the governing agency that finances much of the heart disease research) tends to dispel this notion. The position is taken that failing to exercise regularly can be far more dangerous than by abstaining because one may not be willing to consult a doctor first. In fact, several leaders in the field of public health tend to believe that not seeing a doctor first may be preventing millions of people from beginning an exercise program. Our position is that it is a personal matter as to whether one should consult a physician before embarking on a physical activity program, though doing so is recommended. If a person feels more comfortable by consulting a doctor first, then he or she should do so. It is likely that a physician will recommend the program without restriction, or if a physical problem is found, he or she will likely take steps to correct it and may have suggestions for modifying the program to make it more suitable to the individual.

The second consideration is that a program be individually tailored and one that fits one's own needs and wishes. In other words, if a person is not happy with the program, it will be unlikely that it will meet with success related to his or her personal goals. Each individual must determine which particular approach is best for him or her—specified physical exercises, recreational sports, or a combination of these.

Once you have decided what will make up your exercise program, whether prescribed exercises or recreational sports, you will need to determine how many times a week and the duration of these activities. It is best to avoid the extremes of the "once in a while" or "always without fail." Try to maintain a regular schedule of three to four times a week. It is also a good idea to work out on alternate days—Monday, Wednesday, and Friday, or Tuesday, Thursday, and Saturday. The hour of the day does not necessarily matter. However, it should be remembered that if having decided that your fitness program is going to be high on your priority list of things to do, it should not be difficult to get into the habit of placing regular workouts into your weekly schedule.

Over a number of years controlled studies have provided evidence that physical activity and exercise contributes to one's capacity to reduce stress. Because of its psychological and physiological benefits, exercise is an ideal stress reduction technique for most people. It is accompanied by reduction in anxiety, depression, and anger—three common psychological stress symptoms. Exercise also improves several other psychological stress symptoms by enhancing the participant's vigor and mental alertness. In addition, regular exercise reduces several physiological stress symptoms such as elevated heart rate, blood pressure, and general muscle tension.

In conclusion, a personal system of stress management for athletes, coaches, and athletic directors includes the observance of beneficial health practices. As with any person, the health considerations discussed above are integral in such a system for those involved in intercollegiate athletics.

Chapter 7

Reducing Stress Through Relaxation

"Why don't you just relax?" How many times have you spoken or heard this expression? Although it is frequently used to mean "take it easy," or "slow down," those using the expression are often not aware of its plenary and real meaning. Most of us need some sort of relaxation to relieve the tensions encountered in daily living and this is especially true in the athletics environment.

The purpose of this chapter is to explore various components of relaxation and the conditions that tend to produce a relaxed state. There are numerous procedures and techniques that can help improve a person's ability to relax, and thus reduce stress. It should be kept in mind that what may be satisfactory and effective for one person may not be so for another.

The preceding chapter was concerned with human health practices that can reduce stress. In this chapter the specific and important stress reduction technique of relaxation is discussed in some depth.

The percentage of those in our surveys who used muscle relaxation as a means of reducing stress were: athletes—25 percent, coaches—17 percent, and athletic directors—12 percent.

It is interesting to note that many coaches professed that they tended to suffer headaches during stressful situations. In the general population, four out of five headache conditions are said to be due to muscle tension. If one can recognize when muscles are starting to contract and how to develop control over this by inducing relaxation, it will be very effective, not only in eliminating headaches, but many other stress-related concerns as well.

THE MEANING OF RELAXATION

The reality of muscle fibers is that they have a response repertoire of one. All they can do is contract and this is the response they make to the electrochemical stimulation of impulses carried via the motor nerves. Relaxation is the removal of this stimulation.[1]

The term relaxation response was introduced several years ago by Herbert Benson of Harvard University.[2] This is said to be a natural process and involves a number of bodily changes that occur in the organism when one experiences deep muscle relaxation. This is a physiological response against bodily "overstress," which brings on changes and thus brings the body back into a healthier state and balance. Thus, the basic purpose of any kind of relaxation technique should be to induce the relaxation response.

From the point of view of the physiologist, relaxation is sometimes considered as "zero activity," or as nearly zero as one can manage in the neuromuscular system. That is, it is a neuromuscular accomplishment that results in reduction, or possible complete absence of muscle tonus in a part of, or in the entire body. A primary value of relaxation lies in lowering brain and spinal cord activity, resulting from a reduction of nerve impulses arising in muscle spindles and other sense endings in muscles, tendons, and joint structures.

The terms *relaxation, refreshment,* and *recreation* are often confused in their meaning. Although all of these factors are important to the well-being of the human body, they should not be used interchangeably to mean the same thing. Refreshment is the result of an improved blood supply to the brain for "refreshment" from central fatigue and to the muscles for the disposition of their waste products. This explains in part why mild muscular activity is good for overcoming the fatigue of sitting (seventh-inning stretch) and for hastening recovery after strenuous exercise (an athlete continuing for a short distance slowly after a race).

Recreation may be described as the experience from which a person emerges with the feeling of being "re-created." No single activity is sure to bring this experience to all members of a group, nor is there assurance that an activity will provide recreation again for a given person because it did so previously. These are more the marks of a psychological than a physiological experience. An important essential requirement for a recreational activity is that it completely engross the individual. That is, it is best achieved when the individual's entire attention is engaged. It is in essence the escape from the disintegrating effects of distraction to the healing effect of totally integrated activity. Experiences that produce this effect may range from a vigorous game of tennis to the reading of a comic strip or a good book.

Some individuals consider recreation and relaxation to be the same, which is not the case. Recreation can be considered a type of mental diversion that can be helpful in relieving tension. While mental and muscular tensions are interrelated, it is in the muscle that the tension state is manifested.

Scientists and authors have proposed numerous techniques which individuals might employ in order to achieve relaxed states. A few of these techniques and procedures are considered in the ensuing discussion.

First, it is important to remember that learning to relax is an acquired skill. That is, it is a skill based on the kinesthetic awareness of feeling *tonus* (the normal degree of contraction present in most muscles, which keeps them always ready to function when needed). Unfortunately, it is a skill that too few of us acquire and practice—probably because we have little awareness of how to achieve it.

One of the first steps in learning to relax is to experience tension. That is, one should be sensitive to tensions that exist in his or her body. This can be accomplished by voluntarily contracting a given muscle group, first very strongly and then less and less. Emphasis should be placed on detecting the signal of tension as the first step in "letting go" (relaxing). This can be repeated through a series of selected muscle groups.

You might wish to try the traditional experiment used to demonstrate this phenomenon. Raise one arm so that the palm of the hand is facing outward away from your face. Now, bend the wrist backward and try to point the fingers back toward your face and down toward your forearm. You should feel some strain at the wrist joint. You should also feel something else in the muscle and this is tension, which is due to the muscle contracting the hand backward. Now, flop the hand forward with the fingers pointing downward and you will have accomplished a selected tension-relaxation cycle.

As in the case of any muscular skill, learning how to relax takes time and one should not expect to achieve complete satisfaction immediately. After one has identified a relaxation technique that he or she feels comfortable with, increased practice will eventually achieve satisfactory results.

PROGRESSIVE RELAXATION

The technique of progressive relaxation was developed by Edmund Jacobson many years ago. It is still the technique most often referred to in the literature and probably the one that has the most widespread application. Jacobson found that people under stress often showed signs of increased muscle tension. The mechanism that was producing increased muscle tension in one part of the body quite likely caused similar responses in other areas of the body. The questions raised were: If increased muscle tension caused an exaggerated reaction to stress, would the reverse be true? Could relaxing muscles diminish disturbing physical and possibly mental responses to stress? Jacobson discovered that if he were able to teach his patients to completely relax all the muscles in their arms and legs, for example, the magnitude of their response was significantly suppressed.[3]

In this technique, the person concentrates on progressively relaxing one muscle group after another. The technique is based on the procedure of comparing the difference between tension and relaxation. That is, as previously mentioned, one senses the feeling of tension in order to achieve the feeling of relaxation.

It has already been said that learning to relax is a skill that you can develop by applying the principles of progressive relaxation. One of the first steps is to be able to identify the various muscle groups and how to tense them so that tension and relaxation can be experienced. However, before making suggestions on how to tense and relax the various muscle groups, there are certain important preliminary measures that need to be taken into account:

1. You must understand that this procedure takes time. The more you practice the more proficient you should be come with the skills.
2. Progressive relaxation is not the kind of activity to be done spontaneously, and you should be prepared to spend from twenty to thirty minutes daily in tensing-relaxing activities.

3. Selecting a particular time of day is important and this is pretty much an individual matter. Some recommendations suggest that progressive relaxation be practiced daily—sometime during the day and again in the evening before retiring. For many people this would be difficult unless one time period was set aside before going to the job in the morning. This could be a good option and might help a person to start the day in a more relaxed state.
4. It is important to find a suitable place to practice the tensing-relaxing activities. Again, this is an individual matter with some preferring a bed or couch and others a comfortable chair.
5. Consideration should be given to the amount of time a given muscle is tensed. You should be sure that you are able to feel the difference between tension and relaxation. This means that tension should be maintained from about four to eight seconds.
6. Breathing is an important concomitant in tensing and relaxing muscles. To begin with, it is suggested that three or more deep breaths be taken and held for about five seconds. This will tend to make for better rhythm in breathing. Controlled breathing makes it easier to relax and it is most effective when it is done deeply and slowly. It is ordinarily recommended that one should inhale deeply when the muscles are tensed and exhale slowly when releasing the muscle.

How to Tense and Relax Various Muscle Groups

Muscle groups may be identified in various ways. The classification given here consists of four different groups: (a) muscles of the head, face, tongue, and neck; (b) muscles of the trunk; (c) muscles of the upper extremities; and (d) muscles of the lower extremities.

Muscles of the Head, Face, Tongue, and Neck

There are two chief muscles of the head, one covering the back of the head and one covering the front of the skull. There are about thirty muscles of the face including muscles of the orbit and eyelids, mastication, lips, tongue, and neck. (Incidentally, it has been estimated that it takes twenty-six facial muscles to frown and a proportionately much smaller number to smile.)

Muscles of this group may be tensed and relaxed as follows (relaxing is accomplished by "letting go" after tensing):

1. Raise your eyebrows by opening the eyes as wide as possible. You might wish to look into a mirror to see if you have formed wrinkles on the forehead.
2. Tense the muscles on either side of your nose as if you were going to sneeze.
3. Dilate or flare out the nostrils.
4. Force an extended smile from "ear to ear," while at the same time clenching your teeth.
5. Pull one corner of your mouth up and then the other down.
6. Draw your chin as close to your chest as possible.
7. Do the opposite of the above trying to draw your head back as close to your back as possible.

Muscles of the Trunk

Included in this group are the muscles of the back, chest, abdomen, and pelvis. Here are ways you can tense some of these muscles:

1. Bring your chest forward and at the same time put your shoulders back with emphasis on bringing your shoulder blades as close together as possible.
2. Try to round your shoulders and bring them up to your ears at the same time as you try to bring your neck downward.
3. Give your shoulders a shrug trying to bring them up to your ears at the same time as you try to bring your neck downward.
4. Breathe deeply and hold it momentarily and then blow out the air from your lungs rapidly.
5. Draw in your stomach so that your chest is out beyond your stomach. Exert your stomach muscles by forcing out to make it look like you are fatter in that area than you are.

Muscles of the Upper Extremities

This group includes the muscles of the hands, forearms, upper arms, and shoulders. A number of muscles situated in the trunk may be grouped with the muscles of the upper extremities, their function being to attach the upper limbs to the trunk and move the shoulders and arms. In view of this, there is some overlapping in this and the preceding muscle group. The following are some ways to tense some of these muscles:

1. Clench the fist and then open the hand, extending the fingers as far as possible.
2. Raise one arm shoulder high and parallel to the floor. Bend at the elbow and bring the hand in toward the shoulder. Try to touch your shoulders while attempting to move the shoulder away from the hand. Flex the biceps of the opposite arm in the same manner.
3. Stretch one arm out to the side of the body and try to point the fingers backward toward the body. Repeat this procedure with the other arm.
4. Hold the arm out the same way as above, but this time have the palm facing up and point the fingers inward toward the body. Do the same with the other arm.
5. Stretch one arm out to the side, clench the fist and roll the wrist around slowly. Repeat with the other arm.

Muscles of the Lower Extremities

This group includes muscles of the hips, thighs, legs, feet, and buttocks. The following are ways to tense some of these muscles:

1. Hold one leg at a time out straight, point your toes as far forward as you can. Do the same with the other leg.
2. Do the same, but point your toes as far backward as you can.
3. Turn each foot outward as far as you can and release. Do just the opposite by turning the foot inward as far as you can.
4. Try to draw the thigh muscles up so that you can see the form of the muscles.
5. Make your buttocks tense by pushing down if you are sitting in a chair. If you are lying down try to draw the muscles of the buttocks in close by attempting to force the cheeks together.

These suggestions include several options for tensing various muscles of the body. As you practice them, you will also discover other ways to tense and then let go. A word of caution might be that, in the early stages, you should be alert to the possibility of cramping certain muscles. This can happen particularly with those muscles that are not frequently used. This means that at the beginning you should proceed carefully. It might be a good idea to keep a record of your sessions so that you can refer to these experiences if this might be necessary. This will also help you get into each new session by reviewing your experiences in previous sessions.

Tense *and* Let Go *Activities for Stressful Situations*

What can the football coach on the sidelines, the basketball coach on the bench, the athletic director in the press box, or the athlete in the midst of a difficult test in class do to deal with a stressful situation in the immediate environment? The following examples are recommended and can be performed in a more or less subtle manner and not necessarily be noticed by others:

1. *Hand and Head Press.* Interweave fingers and place hands at the back of the head with elbows pointing out. Push the head backward on the hands while simultaneously pulling the head forward with the hands. Although this can be done while standing, it can also be done while sitting at a desk or table and is less conspicuous.
2. *Wall Press.* Stand with the back against the wall. Allow the arms to hang down at the sides. Turn hands toward the wall and press the wall with the palms, keeping the arms straight (perhaps a useful activity when the boss has your "back to the wall").
3. *Hand Pull.* Bend the right elbow and bring the right hand in with the palm up close to the front of the body. Put the left hand in the right hand. Try to curl the right arm upward while simultaneously resisting with the left hand. Repeat, using the opposite pressure. This can be done while standing or sitting at a desk or table.
4. *Hand Push.* The hands are clasped with the palms together close to the chest with the elbows pointing out. Press the hands together firmly.

5. *Leg Press.* While sitting at a desk or table, cross the left ankle over the right ankle. The feet are on the floor and the legs are at about a right angle. Try to straighten the right leg while resisting with the left leg. Repeat with the right ankle over the left ankle.

6. *The Gripper.* Place one hand in the other and grip hard. Another variation is to grip an object. While standing, this could be the back of a chair, or while sitting, it could be the arms of a chair or the seat.

7. *Chair Push.* While sitting at a desk or table with the hands on the armrests of the chair, push down with the hands. The entire buttocks can be raised from the chair seat. One or both feet can be lifted off the floor, or both can remain in contact with the floor.

8. *Hip Lifter.* While sitting, lift one buttock after the other from the chair seat. Try to keep the head from moving. The hands can be placed at the sides of the chair seat for balance.

9. *Heel and Toe.* From a standing position, rise on the toes. Come back down on the heels while raising both the toes and the balls of the feet.

10. *Fist Clencher.* Clench fists and then open the hands extending the fingers as far as possible.

This short list is comprised of representative examples of what can actually be called *stress exercises*. While we have recommended that these can be performed easily in specific stressful environments, it is obvious that they can be performed elsewhere as well.

THE QUIETING REFLEX

The Quieting Reflex (QR) Concept was discovered several years ago by the distinguished scientist Charles F. Stroebel. This was an outgrowth of his work using biofeedback to treat stress disorders in a clinic population ranging from age seven to seventy. His staff was amazed at the ease with which young members of the population acquired body skills that older patients found increasingly difficult with age. This was particularly true in the transfer and application into the real world with its inevitable stresses and worries.

Initially, the six-second QR was designed to help adults not "just relax," but to automatically adjust their body tension up and down to meet the actual stress at hand. After six months of application/ practice, QR remarkably increased their ability to avoid and eliminate stress and ultimately resulting stress illnesses.

QR is designed to teach people an important life skill, namely, the Quieting Reflex. It can help them live more productive, less stressful lives while at the same time enhancing their healthiness and their potential by reducing the negative effects of inappropriately perceived stress. Thus, the purpose of the QR program is to help individuals approach the unavoidable demands of life in a way in which they can feel better about themselves and others and to live less stressful lives.

The fight or flight response, which was discussed previously, is similar to the passing gear in a car. The passing gear is a wonderful emergency safety mechanism. When you get into a tight spot, you can push the accelerator to the floor and zoom out of the problem. At the same time, if you drive your car in passing gear all the time, it creates profound wear and tear on the car. Obviously, this is not a very effective way to use an automobile. The same is true for our bodies. We should not stay in passing gear unnecessarily. This is especially good advice for coaches, athletes, and athletic directors.

The problem with many people is that they learn how to overuse the passing gear and eventually they do not know how to get out of passing gear. Simply telling a person "not to worry" or "just take it easy" is not satisfactory because most people do not understand what it means to "just relax," nor do they know how to "not worry." The common statement, "Don't worry. Be happy" is not a goal that can be easily achieved by most individuals.

For the most part, stressful situations require mental rather than an intense-physical (caveman) type of response. Yet people often use their fight or flight reaction in the absence of immediate physical threat. Inappropriate use of the fight or flight emergency response lessens the mental alertness people need to solve whatever problem is causing stress. This overuse of the fight or flight response is clearly inappropriate and maladaptive.

Many individuals inadvertently learn to activate the emergency response at the slightest sign and therefore repeatedly use this mechanism inappropriately. This panic reaction may then prevent them from performing appropriately—and also prevent them from responding from within their true potential. In other words, the stress reaction acts as a block of learning, optimum response, and other life pursuits (actual laboratory body measurements of individuals indicate that most of them have a quick panic reaction, lasting from six to ten seconds, and this reduces their ability to perform optimally).

Many individuals develop or maintain a high level of arousal and do so more frequently and for longer periods than they should, as often is the case with some coaches and athletes. Bodies of healthy people should quickly recover normal balance after their initial reaction to stress. This is the body's inherent quieting reaction, or Quieting Reflex. However, many individuals have unconsciously taught their bodies to override their own natural quieting responses until constant tension, anxiety and tightness begin to seem normal to them.

What the QR program is all about is a contrary response to the passing gear or emergency reaction. This contrary response is called the Quieting Reflex. It begins in early training phases as a response to things that get on people's nerves, that annoy them, or that get them frustrated or angry. With progressive practice, individuals *can acquire a virtually reflexive ability* to produce a set of behaviors that are actually contrary to the inappropriate use of the passing gear. The two states obviously cannot happen simultaneously, so there has now been produced a new adaptive state where individuals do not have to get their bodies upset and reactive when it is not appropriate or productive.

The emergency reaction involves approximately five steps. The first is increased vigilance or paying attention to what is potentially harmful in the environment—that is, to whatever is feared. Frequently and almost simultaneously there is a blush reaction, a wetness of the hands, or a tendency toward perspiration. Almost simultaneously comes a perking of attention and a tension of the musculature of the face. The face becomes firm or grim. At about three seconds into this passing gear emergency response, there is a catching or holding of the breath or there is shallow, quick breathing, almost panting. The next change frequently is a drop in hand temperature. The hands and often the feet become cold and clammy. And, finally the jaw is clenched. These changes have been specifically measured by laboratory instrumentation.

The Quieting Reflex is a reversal of these steps. The first thing that happens in the Quieting Reflex is that the person becomes aware that something is annoying him or her, making him or her tense or anxious. They learn how to monitor their body to determine what cues trigger this emergency response and then he or she learns a systematic way to reverse the emergency reaction by eliciting the Quieting Reflex. Thus, instead of being dependent upon tranquilizers, alcohol or other substances, young people and adults can use the 6-second technique as a way of keeping their bodies calm when they are not really required to "tense up"—or "stand their ground and fight or run away."

It has been found that QR training helps people regain the capacity they had as younger children to recover quickly from excessive stress. In the course of training, young people and others learn to recognize when they are overreacting to stress and learn specific techniques to bring their bodies back to a healthy level of activity. Later in training, they learn to apply these skills consciously in day-to-day school or job situations. Eventually through repeated practice the quieting technique becomes the body's automatic and unconscious response to stressful situations. When an emergency response is inappropriate, the body automatically responds with a QR.

It has also been found that a great majority of individuals, as they become proficient in evoking the Quieting Reflex, gain a new sense of freedom. They recognize that many of the problems that have disturbed them in the past are not beyond their voluntary control. Their new sense of mastery with QR leads to an enhanced self-concept and an ability to use their full potential in ways that they previously found to be impossible.[4]

MENTAL PRACTICE AND IMAGERY
IN RELAXATION

Mental practice is a symbolized rehearsal of a physical activity in the absence of any overt muscular movement. This means that a person imagines in his or her own mind the way he or she will perform a given activity. *Imagery* is concerned with the development of a mental image that may aid one in the performance of an activity. In mental practice, the person thinks through what he or she is going to do and with the imagery he or she may suggest to himself or herself (or another may suggest a condition to him or her) and he or she then tries to effect a mental image of the condition.

The use of mental practice in performing motor skills is not new. In fact, research in this general area has been carried out for well over half a century. This research has revealed that imagining a movement will likely produce recordable electric action potential emanating from the muscle groups that would be called up if the movement were to be actually carried out. In addition, most mental activity is accompanied by general rises in muscular tension—an initial step in preparedness for action.

One procedure in the use of mental practice for relaxation is that of making suggestions to oneself. In early childhood, we first learn to act on the basis of verbal instructions from others. Later we learn to guide and direct our own behavior on the basis of our own language activities—we literally talk to ourselves, giving ourselves instructions. This point of view has long been supported by research that postulates that speech as a form of communication between children and adults later becomes a means of organizing the child's own behavior. That is, the function that was previously divided between two people—child and adult—becomes an internal function of human behavior. An example of this approach follows:

> I am going to relax completely. First, I will relax my forehead and scalp. I will let all the muscles of my forehead and scalp relax and become completely at rest. All the wrinkles will come out of my forehead and that part of my body will relax completely. Now, I will relax the muscles of my face. I will just let them relax and go limp. There will be no tension in my jaw. Next, I will relax my neck muscles. (This is continued for all of the muscle groups of the body from head to toe.)

Another way imagery can be used to promote a relaxed state is by making comparative statements such as "float like a feather," or "melt like ice." Creative persons (such as yourself) will be able to think of many such comparative statements to assist in producing a relaxed state.

All of the relaxation procedures in this chapter have been used with varying degrees of success when appropriately applied. However, it is important to repeat that what may be satisfactory for one person may not necessarily be effective for another.

The following two chapters will deal with meditation and biofeedback as means of inducing the relaxation response. In this regard it is important that some attention be given to the underlying theories of progressive relaxation, meditation, and biofeedback. In progressive relaxation, it is theorized that if the muscles of the body are relaxed, the mind in turn will be quieted. In the practice of meditation it is believed that if the mind is quieted, then other systems of the body will tend to be more readily stabilized. In biofeedback the theoretical basis tends to suggest some sort of integration of progressive relaxation and meditation. It is believed that the brain has the potential for voluntary control over all the systems it monitors and is itself also affected by all of these systems. Thus, it is the intimacy of interaction between mind and body that has provided the mechanism through which one can learn voluntary control over biological activity.

In summary, all of the techniques for stress avoidance or release are concerned with mind-body interactions and all of them are designed to induce the relaxation response described at the beginning of the chapter. These techniques can be particularly relevant to athletes, coaches, and athletic administrators who frequently find themselves exposed to stress-inducing circumstances.

Chapter 8

Reducing Stress Through Meditation

The percentage of those in our surveys who used meditation as a means of coping with stress were as follows: athletes—15 percent, coaches—3 percent, and athletic directors—13 percent. The figures for athletes and athletic directors is much higher than for those of other populations, which is usually from 2 to 4 percent. A possible reason for this is that the athletes and athletic directors in our studies perceived meditation differently than the scientific concept of it. That is, many of them thought of meditation as "just sitting and resting." (Interestingly, some individuals feel that this practice can achieve the same results as meditation. This could possibly be true for some people, while others may obtain more effective results with a more scientific and thorough practice of meditation.)

The Eastern practice of meditation dates back more than 2,000 years. Until recently, this ancient practice has been encumbered with religious as well as cultural connotations. In the 1960s, countercultures began using it to achieve a more natural means of living and relaxing. Today, persons from all walks of life can be counted among peoples around the world who practice and realize the positive effects that meditation can have upon the human mind and body. This chapter will discuss various aspects of meditation: (a) types of meditation, (b) information about a procedure that can be easily learned and practiced for the purpose of reducing stress, and (c) some scientific evidence that supports the use of meditation as a stress reduction technique.

It has been asserted by Kenneth Pelletier[1] that meditation should be defined as an experimental exercise involving an individual's actual attention, not his or her belief systems or other cognitive processes, and that it should not be confused with prolonged, self-induced lethargy. The nervous system needs intensity and variety and external stimulation to maintain proper functioning.

Robert Woolfolk and Frank Richardson[2] have suggested that at the very least meditation can give the mind a rest—a brief vacation from stress and worry, one that requires neither a travel agent nor days free from the responsibility of work or family. It is almost as though meditation allows us to temporarily shut down those information-processing mechanisms of the brain that are ultimately responsible for producing stress. In addition, this short vacation from stress rests and revitalizes our coping abilities and gives us a more balanced outlook and increased energy for dealing with the difficulties that face us.

Although there are many meditation techniques, *concentration* is an important factor contributing to success in most of them. The mind's natural flow from one idea to another is quieted by the individual's concentration. Lowering mental activity may be an easy task, but almost total elimination of random thoughts takes a great deal of time and practice on the part of the person seeking to practice meditation.

This pertinent question is often raised: Are sleep and meditation the same thing? Sleep has been likened to meditation, as both are hypometabolic states, that is, restful states where the body experiences decreased metabolism. But meditation is not a form of sleep. Although some similar psychological changes have been found in sleep and meditation, they are not the same and one is not a substitute for the other. In this regard, it is interesting to note that various studies have shown that meditation may restore more energy than sleep.

Countless positive pronouncements have been made about meditation. These have emanated from some of the most notable scientists who have spent a good portion of their time studying and researching stress. In fact, the scientific community has discovered many of the positive effects that the repeated practice of meditation has upon those who are stress ridden. Various scientific studies have shown that meditation can actually decrease the possibilities of an individual contracting stress-related disorders, and that mediators have a much faster recovery rate when exposed to a stressful situation than nonmeditators. Specifically, from a physiological point of view, Herbert Benson[3] has found that meditation decreases the body's metabolic rate with the following decreases in bodily function involved: oxygen consumption; breathing rate; heart rate and blood pressure; sympathetic nervous system activity; and blood lactate (a chemical produced in the body during stressful encounters).

Also, meditation tends to increase the psychological ability of those who practice it, as well as to reduce anxiety. Research indicates that meditation can be a path to better health (later in this chapter we will examine some of this scientific inquiry in more detail.)

TYPES OF MEDITATION

More than twenty meditational systems are known. Interestingly enough, although there are many meditation techniques, research tends to show that one technique is about as good as another for improving the way we handle stress. We have arbitrarily selected four types of meditation for discussion here: (1) Christian meditation, (2) meditative running, (3) strategic meditation, and (4) transcendental meditation.

Christian Meditation

If you ask the average person about meditation the response will ordinarily be that it is concerned with "sitting and thinking," or "engaging in silent prayer." And, this is essentially what Christian meditation means. According to Herbert Benson, the roots of Christian meditation can be explained as follows:

> Christian meditation and mysticism were well developed within the Byzantine church and known as Hesychasm. Hesychasm involved a method or repetitive prayer which was described in the fourteenth century at Mount Athos in Greece by Gregory of Sinai and was called "The Prayer of the Heart" or "The Prayer of Jesus." It dates back to the beginnings of Christianity. The prayer itself was called secret meditation and was transmitted from older to younger monks through an initiation rite.[3]

In modern times this ritual is not so pronounced and one feels he or she is meditating by reflecting upon certain experiences and evaluating certain activities that have taken place in his or her life. This frequently includes exercises of prayer and scripture readings—with widespread reports of stress release, peace of mind and personal renewal.

Meditative Running

Two prominent researchers, Diane and Robert Hales,[4] have reported on a concept that encompasses a combination of meditation and running and what we would consequently describe as meditative running. Although running and meditation seem like completely opposite states—one strenuous and the other serene—both can be considered as paths to altered states of consciousness, and together they can profoundly affect both body and mind. It is interesting that exercisers who meditate as they work out, often literally change the way their heart and lungs function. They burn less oxygen and use energy more efficiently. It is known that Tibetan monks, using a similar approach and concentrating on a mantra, have run distances of 200 miles over mountain trails in less than thirty hours.

The Hales also reported on the work of Earl Solomon, a psychiatrist at Harvard Medical School, and his research assistant, Ann Bumpus, who adapted Benson's meditation technique so that the runner can elicit the relaxation response with eyes open and feet moving. In their method they suggest the following:

1. Run at a gentle pace.
2. Deeply relax all muscles.
3. Breathe in, breathe out sharply through the mouth.
4. Repeat a mantra as you exhale.
5. Let relaxation come at its own pace.
6. Overcome distracting thoughts by focusing on a mantra.
7. If running outdoors, remain aware of any external danger, such as approaching vehicles.

Strategic Meditation

Amarjit S. Sethi,[5] one of the contributors to the series on *Stress in Modern Society*, has developed the concept of strategic meditation.

He defines it as a process of balancing "calculative thinking" and "noncalculative thinking." In order to give specificity to this concept he has labeled it "strategic meditation" so that it may be distinguished from other forms of meditation. The meditational process takes place in different contexts, comprising both the facts and the values of a given environment. The study of interactions between facts and values in shaping calculative and noncalculative thinking becomes a process of strategic meditation. It is strategic because meditation examines problems, identifies their nature, and establishes perspective. It is meditational because a person transforms the problem-solving orientation through a focus on both the problem and its solution—and this begins to suggest elements of how an individual processes information in a relatively "problem-free context" that has been termed noncalculative. Another term for such a level of consciousness is playfulness—a type of transcendent activity. The emphasis, in a meditational exercise, shifts from complex calculation and sophisticated decision rules to selective perception, leading to a problem-free context.

To practice strategic meditation one needs to develop his or her own diagnosis of the perceived problem. Problem solving is utilized as a process of investigating the source of stress, and is also integrated as a part of the meditational process. This phase involves perception of the environment, analysis of the problem, and design of alternative solutions. The problem-solving process is therefore integrated with a meditational process.

Transcendental Meditation

Of the various types of meditation, transcendental meditation (TM) is perhaps the best known. It was introduced in the United States many years ago by Maharishi Mahesh Yogi. It is believed that he used the term transcendental (a literal meaning of which is "going beyond") to indicate that it projects one beyond the level of a wakeful experience to a state of profound rest along with heightened alertness.

TM involves the repetition of a *mantra* (a word or specific sound) for fifteen to twenty minutes daily with the meditator in a relaxed position with eyes closed. Those who have practiced TM attest to its positive effects. While other forms of meditation may have unique procedures, it is safe to say that many derive in some way from basic TM. The discussion that follows is based in part on this type of meditation.

A PROCEDURE FOR MEDITATING

Presented here is a description of a procedure for meditating that has met with much success. Certain basic considerations should be taken into account. The following descriptive list of these considerations is general in nature. The reader can make his or her own specific application as best fits individual needs and interests.

1. Locate a Quiet Place and Assume a Comfortable Position

The importance of a quiet environment should be obvious since concentration is facilitated in a tranquil surrounding. The position that a person may assume for meditation is an individual matter. However, when it is suggested that one assume a comfortable position, this might be amended by, "but not too comfortable." If one is too comfortable it is possibile to fall asleep, and this of course would compromise the purpose of meditation. It is best not to totally recline while meditating.

A position might be taken that allows some latitude for gentle movement. This freedom of movement can provide for a comfortable posture and, at the same time, guard against the individual "falling into dreamland." The main consideration is that the person be in a comfortable enough position to remain this way for a period of fifteen minutes or so. One such position is to sit on the floor with legs crossed with the back straight, resting on the legs and buttocks. The head should be erect and the hands resting in the lap. If you prefer to sit in a chair rather than on the floor, select a chair with a straight back. You need to be the judge of comfort and you should select a position where you feel you are able to concentrate and remain in this position for a period of time.

2. Focus Your Concentration

As mentioned before, concentration is the essential key to successful meditation. If you focus on one specific thing, such as an object or a sound or a personal feeling, it is less likely that your thoughts will be distracted. You might want to consider focusing on such things as a fantasy trip, reexperiencing a trip already taken, a place that has not been visited, or a certain sound or repeated phrase, chant, or prayer.

3. Use a Nonsense Word or Phrase

Some techniques of meditation, such as the popular transcendental meditation, involve the chanting of a particular word (mantra) as one meditates. While the mantra has important meaning for the meditator, we refer to it as a nonsense word because it should be devoid of any connotation that would send one thinking in many directions and hinder concentration.

4. Be Aware of Natural Breathing Rhythm

The importance of natural breathing rhythm should not be underestimated. In fact, some clinical psychologists recommend this as a means of concentrating. That is, one can count the number of times he or she inhales and exhales, and this in itself is a relaxing mental activity. Plenary, relaxed breathing is generally considered to be optimum.

5. The Time for Meditation

Since meditation is an activity to quiet the mind it is strongly recommended that the practice not be undertaken immediately at the end of the day. At this time, the mind may be in a very active state of reviewing the day's activities. One practice would be to engage in a fifteen- to twenty-minute period in the morning and another such period in the evening preferably before dinner, or possibly two hours after dinner.

With the above considerations in mind, you should be ready to experiment. To begin with, assume a comfortable position in a quiet place with as passive an attitude as possible. Try to dismiss all wandering thoughts from your mind and concentrate on a relaxed body while keeping the eyes closed. When feeling fairly relaxed, the repetition of a word or phrase can begin. This can be repeated orally or silently. Repeat your own chosen word or phrase in this manner over and over, keeping the mind clear of any passing thoughts. At first, this may be very difficult, but with practice it becomes easier. Christian meditation will differ in the content and sequence of the repetition that might be used.

After a period of about fifteen or twenty minutes (or less if you wish) discontinue repetition of the word or phrase. Become aware of your relaxed body once again. Give yourself a few moments before moving, as your body will need to readjust. For successful prolonged results one might consider continuing the practice two times daily for fifteen to twenty minutes.

If you have difficulty trying to meditate on your own, it is possible to seek the services of an experienced meditator for assistance and supervision. The recent more widespread popularity of meditation has been accompanied by the establishment of meditation centers and also Christian meditation and prayer groups in some communities.

SCIENTIFIC EVIDENCE SUPPORTING THE BENEFITS OF MEDITATION

Since many people are not aware of the value of meditation and since many others suspect it as a rather unorthodox procedure, it seems fitting to impress upon the reader that it is an important area of scientific research.

The phenomenon of meditation is not an easy one to study objectively. One of the primary reasons for this is that it is extremely difficult to control all of the variables inherent in a given situation. For example, the difference in the length of meditation sessions as well as the degree of meditating experience of the subjects sometimes militates against obtaining researchable experimental and control groups. These limitations should be kept in mind when reading the following research reports. It should also be remembered that more than 500 research studies in this area have been undertaken since 1970. Those cited here are merely representative examples of this vast number.

In studying meditation as an intervention in stress reactivity, Goleman and Schwartz[6] used skin conductive measures (a process similar to the polygraph or lie detector) to study certain aspects of meditation. There were sixty subjects, thirty of whom had over two years of experience with TM. The other thirty were nonmeditators. The subjects were randomly selected for participation in one of three conditions: (a) meditation, (b) relaxation with eyes open, and (c) relaxation with eyes closed. In the meditation group, both meditators and nonmeditators were assigned. The meditators with experience engaged in TM, and those without experience (controls) were instructed in a simple version of TM. After practicing this for a period of twenty minutes, subjects were instructed to open their eyes and view a five-minute film designed to be used as a stressor. During meditation and while viewing the film, the subjects were measured for skin conductance and pulse rate. These measurements were recorded twice each minute. Experienced meditators showed more increase in skin conductance during the time immediately before the highly emotionally charged part of the film. However, a decrease in this measurement occurred after the film was viewed. These results could be interpreted to mean generally that those experienced in the practice of meditation can relieve stress more readily by using this particular medium.

In studying the physiological effects of meditation, Wallace[7] used subjects who had practiced meditation for a period of six months to three years. The subjects sat with eyes open for five minutes. This was followed by a fifteen-minute period with closed eyes, and then for a half-hour period they used TM. At the end of this time, they sat with closed eyes for ten minutes followed by open eyes for five minutes.

Several physiological measurements were recorded during TM and the control periods. For the experimental period (TM), oxygen consumption was reduced by 16 percent. In addition, a 14 percent reduction in carbon dioxide elimination occurred. These results were interpreted to mean that slowed metabolic rate and a state of deep rest were evident.

The researcher also made a comparison of the oxygen consumption reduction during meditation and then during a night's sleep. This amounted to a difference of about 9 percent. This seemed to justify a generalization that twenty minutes of meditation produced nearly two times the metabolic decrease than that which occurred during sleep. This could also be interpreted to mean that a deep state of relaxation could be obtained in a relatively short period of time by use of meditation.

Since much credence has been placed on stress reduction in the control of and resistance to disease, it seems appropriate to look at the specific technique of meditation in that regard also. Considering that the health of one's gums is is assumed by some researchers to be an acceptable criterion for overall health, and further, that gum inflammation seems related to stress levels, this condition appears to be a satisfactory medium for studying the general area of disease resistance. Klemons[8] undertook a study of this nature by examining forty-six practicing meditators for common inflammation of the gums before and after a special course involving extended meditation. Significant improvement was reported for the meditators when compared to a control group of nonmeditators. A conclusion was drawn from this microindicator study that a TM program increases resistance to disease if, as mentioned previously, the condition gum inflammation can be accepted as a valid criterion/indicator.

An interesting study regarding reaction time and meditation was conducted by Shaw and Kolb.[9] Reaction time is the amount of time it takes from the time a signal is given until the initial movement (stimulus response). This should not be confused with speed of movement, which is concerned with how fast the initial movement is completed. (Reaction time and speed of movement are important factors in most aspects of athletic performance.)

In this study, the subjects were nine meditators with a like number of nonmeditators as controls. All subjects reacted to a signal that was a flash of light. At this stimulus the subjects responded by pressing a button. The results showed that meditators tended to react faster than nonmeditators by almost a 30 percent difference. Following such stimulus-response trails, all subjects took a fifteen-minute break period. During this time the meditators practiced TM and the nonmeditators sat with eyes closed. On a retest of both groups, the meditators' reaction time was *reduced* 15 percent while the nonmeditators' reaction time *increased* by about 10 percent.

Various generalizations could be drawn from this study. For example, one could perhaps conclude that practicing meditation could improve coordination of functions related to mind and body.

In another study, Kirsch and Henry[10] asked thirty-eight speech-anxious subjects to give a speech and their heart rates were assessed immediately before the speeches were given. They were assigned the following treatment strategies: systematic desensitization; desensitization and meditation replacing progressive relaxation; meditation only; and no treatment. All three treatment manuals included coping-skills instructions. The results indicated that the three treatments were equally effective in reducing anxiety and produced greater reduction in self-reported (but not behavioral) anxiety than that found in untreated subjects.

It was found that *expectancy* for improvement may have been a more important factor than coping devices themselves in reducing stress. The lack of significant differences between treatment groups suggests the viability of considering self-administered training in meditation, coupled with coping-skills instructions, as an alternative to self-administered desensitization programs. (Note: Systematic self-desensitization as a stress-reducing technique will be dealt with in Chapter 10.)

Hall and Goldstein[11] evaluated the effects of a behavioral approach (consisting of a relaxation exercise and meditational imagery) to disease by measuring selected physiological aspects of immune responsiveness in cancer patients. The exercise involved patients imagining that feeble cancer cells were crushed by stalwarts of the immune system. It was found that behavioral therapy amplified the immune system's response to disease. In physiological terms, it accelerated the rate of which lymphocytes mobilized to attack foreign bodies and possibly increased their own numbers. Although this study needs to be confirmed by further research, it does point to a correlation between meditation (mental states) and immunity. Other studies have shown that the presence of a strong and persistent religious faith may decrease the incidence of stress and disease and also can shorten the recovery periods from surgery and illness.

In a study to determine the influence of meditation on the increased orderliness of thinking, Miskiman[12] used two groups of subjects: one of meditators and a control group that relaxed twice daily with closed eyes. After the first forty days of the TM program, the meditators increased appreciably in their tendency to spontaneously organize memorized material in their minds. This was measured by the Index of Cluster In Recall. Members of the control group did not change significantly. Also, the organization of memory in meditators was stronger and more stable over a period of two to six months than was the case in the control group. The memories of the meditators decreased only 3 percent in recall efficiency while the memories of the nonmeditators decreased 38 percent.

In an interesting study, Tojoa[13] tried to determine the effect of meditation on intelligence. One year after fourteen of the subjects began a TM program, he used the seven most regular meditators among them for the experimental group, with the control group consisting of nonmeditators. He administered a neuroticism test and an intelligence test, with the result showing significant decrease in neuroticism and an increase in intelligence in the experimental group and no significant changes in the nonmeditating control group. (It should be remembered that the difference was in an improved intelligence test score, which in itself is not necessarily a guarantee of improved intelligence in general.)

Finally, a study by Morse and colleagues[14] should be of particular interest to college student-athletes. These researchers found that meditation is an effective means of coping with test anxiety and improving test performance.

The studies reported here comprise only a bare minimum of the large number that have been undertaken in the area of effectiveness of meditation. In all cases, these examples have shown positive effects of meditation. However, it is repeated that certain precautions need to be taken into account in interpreting the results, and the reader is reminded again of the possible limitations that were mentioned at the outset of this discussion.

Chapter 9

Reducing Stress Through Biofeedback

As most populations, the respondents in our surveys infrequently used biofeedback as a stress-reducing technique. Perhaps the major reason for this is a lack of familiarity with biofeedback techniques and procedures. The percent of those using it were athletes—1.5 percent, coaches—less than 1 percent, and athletic directors—2 percent.

Although literature on the subject is not as abundant as in other areas, one report suggests that athletes in an identified group have been trained to maximize athletic performance using biofeedback.[1] In this instance, the members of the Canadian military biathlon team underwent biofeedback training in addition to regular training to maximize their performance in the sport that combines cross-country skiing with rifle target shooting. The team members were trained to lower their arousal rapidly after a period of racing and to squeeze the trigger only between heartbeats. As a result, the Canadian biathletes went from being perennially modest achievers to world champions.

In our discussion of biofeedback, it should be made clear that we are addressing a complex and complicated subject. It will be our purpose to discuss this phenomenon in terms of what it is claimed to be and also what it is intended to do. It should be kept in mind that, at least in the early stages of biofeedback training (BFT), an important factor is that it takes place under qualified supervision. This means that anyone wishing to participate in BFT should seek the services of one trained in this area.

THE MEANING OF BIOFEEDBACK

The term *feedback* has been used in various frames of reference. It may have been used originally in engineering in connection with control systems that involve feedback procedures. These feedback control systems make adjustments to environmental changes, such as the case of your thermostat controlling temperature levels in your home based on its continuous monitoring of those temperatures.

Learning theorists use the term feedback interchangeably with the expression *knowledge of results,* to describe the process of providing the learner with information with reference to how accurate his or her reactions were. In other words, feedback is knowledge of various kinds that the performer received about his or her performance. (Coaches, for example, use video tapes to provide feedback of players' athletic performance.) With particular reference to *motor skill learning,* some psychologists have reported that feedback in the form of *knowledge of results* is the strongest, *most important variable controlling performance and learning.* Further, studies have repeatedly shown that there is frequently little improvement without such feedback, that there is progressive improvement with it, and deterioration or decline in improvement when feedback is withdrawn. These findings are of great importance for the area of athletic performance.

According to Barbara Brown,[2] one of the foremost authorities and early pioneers on the subject of biofeedback, the terms *feedback* and *feedback control systems* were borrowed by physiologists when they began developing theory regarding how the functions of the body were performed. Modern writers on the subject of biofeedback seem to describe it essentially the same way, although some may elaborate more in determining its precise meaning. That is, some merely state what it is, while others may extend the description to include what it does. For example, one source may describe it as any information that we receive about the functioning of our internal organs such as the heart, sweat glands, muscles, and brain. Another similar description may indicate that it is a process in which information about an organism's biologic activity is supplied for perception by the same organism. Another source may extend this definition by indicating that biofeedback is the monitoring of signals from the body, such as muscle tension and hand warmth, and the feeding of that information back through the use of sophisticated instruments to individuals so that they can get external information regarding precisely what is happening inside their bodies.

It is estimated that the human body contains perhaps millions of individual feedback systems. Information about the external environment is sensed by any of the five senses and relayed to a control center, usually the brain, where it is integrated with other relevant information. When the sensed information is significant enough, central control generates commands for appropriate body changes.

These senses can also be thought of as *perception,* which is concerned with how we obtain information from the environment and what conclusions we draw from the process. Learning theorists agree that the forms of perception most involved in learning are *auditory* perception, *visual* perception, *kinesthetic* perception, and *tactile* perception. Auditory perception is the mental interpretation of what a person hears. Visual perception is the mental interpretation of what a person sees. Kinesthetic perception is the mental interpretation of the sensation of body movement. Tactile perception is the mental interpretation of what a person experiences through the sense of touch. In this connection, it is common practice among scientists in the field of learning to refer to auditory feedback, visual feedback, kinesthetic feedback, and tactile feedback.

BIOFEEDBACK INSTRUMENTATION

We are all aware that the human body itself is a complicated and complex biofeedback instrument, which alerts us to certain internal activity, as mentioned in the previous discussion. However, many students of the subject feel that there is still a need for sensitive instruments to monitor physiological and psychological reactivity. The following text briefly discusses some of the more widely known biofeedback instruments that are used for both research and therapeutic purposes.

Electromyograph (EMG)

Electromyography is the recording of electric phenomena occurring in muscles during contraction. Needle or skin electrodes are used and connected with an oscilloscope so that action potentials may be viewed and recorded. (The oscilloscope is an instrument that visually displays an electrical wave on a fluorescent screen.) This instrumentation, as others, can now be computer enhanced or computer based. Before the electromyograph was available, guesswork ordinarily had to be used to try to determine the participation of the muscles in movement. When a muscle is completely relaxed or inactive, it has no electric potential. However, when it is engaged in contraction, current appears.

It is believed that EMG training can produce deep muscle relaxation and relieve tension. A person gets the feedback by seeing a gauge or hearing a sound from the machine, and he or she knows immediately the extent to which certain muscles are relaxed or tensed. A muscle frequently used in EMG training for research and other purposes is the *frontalis* located in the front of the head.

Another important use of EMG is in retraining a person following an injury or disease when there is a need to observe small increments of gain in function of a muscle.

Feedback Thermometers

The obvious purpose of feedback thermometers is to record body temperatures. Ordinarily, a thermistor is attached to the hands or the fingers. This highly sensitive instrument shows very small increments of degrees of temperature change so that the person receives the information with a visual or auditory signal. This kind of feedback instrumentation has been recommended for such purposes as reduction of stress and anxiety and autonomic nervous system relaxation.

Electroencephalograph (EEG)

The purpose of the electroencephalograph (EEG) is to record amplitude and frequency of brain waves. It has been used in research for many years, and has been successful in helping to diagnose certain clinical diseases. In addition, EEG feedback has found use in psychotherapy and in reducing stress as well as pain.

An interesting horizon for EEG feedback is how it might be involved in the areas of creativity and learning. In fact, some individuals involved in creativity studies have indicated that they can emerge from the EEG *theta* state with answers to problems that they previously were unable to solve. (Perhaps a coach could be tempted to speculate about this use when formulating a game plan.) The theta waves are ordinarily recorded when a person is in a state of drowsiness or actually falling asleep. For this reason the near-sleep condition has been referred to by some as *sleep learning* or by others as *twilight learning.*

Galvanic Skin Response (GSR)

Numerous kinds of galvanic skin response (GSR) instruments are used to measure changes in electrical resistance of the skin to detect emotional arousal. In each case the instrument reacts in proportion to the amount of perspiration one emits and the person is informed of the changes in electrical resistance by an auditory or visual signal. One aspect of GSR is concerned with the use of the polygraph or lie detector, which is intended to record a response that indicates if a person is communicating an untruth. GSR feedback is often recommended for use in relaxation, reducing tension, improvement of ability to sleep, or for emotional control.

In general, the purpose of biofeedback instruments is to provide accurate and reliable data that will increase one's awareness of how the body is functioning and demonstrate one's influence of his or her action on the body. Such information should be useful in motivating an individual to take an active self-interest in his or her own well-being. After such information is received, if it has been obtained under the supervision of a qualified person, there may be a number of sessions arranged for consultation and training. Perhaps the ultimate objective is for the individual to be able to gain increased control over his or her own autonomic nervous system.

Unquestionably, biofeedback has influenced our way of thinking with reference to the capacity of a person to control his or her physiological functions. In view of this, perhaps one of its foremost contributions is that it creates in an individual a feeling of his or her own responsibility for personal well-being. It also has some important obvious implications for stress management among athletes and athletics professionals.[3]

Chapter 10

Reducing Stress Through Self-Modification of Behavior

Again, we will consider *behavior* as anything that the organism does as a result of some kind of stimulation. We will consider the term *modification* to mean a change in the organism caused by environmental factors. Thus, when the two terms are used together—behavior modification—they are interpreted to mean some kind of change in the way a person has ordinarily reacted to specific stimulus or series of stimuli.

It is not uncommon for some individuals to display behavior that directly or indirectly causes stress arousal, either for themselves or for the person/persons toward whom the behavioral action is directed. It is the purpose of this final chapter to provide information that will assist the reader in modifying his or her own behavior for the purpose of correcting, or at least improving, this condition.

The area of behavior modification has become so broad in scope that it is used in many frames of reference. We would like to emphasize at this point that, for our purposes, we are not considering it as a variety of psychological and/or psychiatric techniques (therapist-client relations) for altering behavior. On the contrary, our recommendations for the use of the process of behavior modification are confined to its potential as a means for individuals to reduce certain stress-connected factors involved in their environments. This is to say that if a person can change a behavior that typically provokes a stressful situation, it could be possible to eliminate, or at least minimize the stressful condition. For example, let us say that if a person constantly uses what others consider to be unwarranted criticism, this can create a problem in personal or work relationships and thus a stressful atmosphere.

In general, the practice of behavior modification involves *external assistance* as in the case of a teacher or counselor trying to effect a behavior change in a student or a group of students. This is an exercise in assisting the individual with the direction of modification, with the individual subsequently attempting to improve upon his or her own behavior. This assumes that a person can develop the ability to increase desirable or appropriate behavior and to decrease undesirable or inappropriate behavior. This involves self-control, which can be described as manipulation of environmental events that influence one's own behavior for the purposes of changing the behavior. Self-control can eventually lead to behavioral self-management which is primarily the learning and practice of new habits. Satisfactory self-control and successful self-management are obviously contingent upon some sort of understanding of self, and this is the subject of the ensuing discussion.

TOWARD AN UNDERSTANDING OF SELF

To put an understanding of self in its proper perspective, consideration must be given to the basic aspects of *self-structure* and *self-concept*. Self-structure is the framework of an individual's complex profile of motives, perceptions, cognitions, feelings, and values—the product of developmental processes. Self-structure is revealed in behavior. One reveals in his or her behavior the following aspects of self-structure: knowledge, skills, and interests acquired; the goals he or she is seeking; the beliefs, values, and attitudes adopted; the roles learned; and the self-concept he or she has formed. Thus, self-concept is an aspect of self-structure.

Among the most relevant and significant perceptions that an individual acquires are those of himself or herself in various life situations (self-concept). Further, the self-concept is made up of a large number of percepts, each of which contains one or more qualities to which one personally ascribes. To be more specific, self-percept pertains to sense impressions of a trait one ascribes to himself or herself, while self-concept consists of the totality of one's self-percepts organized in some sort of order.

The frame of reference of self-concept with which we are concerned here involves the total personality concept. A great deal of clinical and experimental evidence indicates that a human being must be considered as a whole and not a collection of parts, and thus a total personality.

But this immediately raises the question: "What comprises the total personality?" Many experts who spend much of their time studying human personality are not always in agreement as to what personality is or how it functions. However, if one were to analyze the literature on the subject it would be found generally that the total personality consists of the sum of all the *physical, social, emotional,* and *intellectual* aspects of any individual. This can also be expressed in terms of the physical self, the social self, the emotional self, and the intellectual self (with everyone manifesting certain kinds of physical behavior, social behavior, emotional behavior, and intellectual behavior). Theologians and Christian counselors also refer to the spiritual dimension of the individual as the spiritual Self, or the spiritual dimension of the total person.

Although this discussion deals with self-concept in a general way, as you read on you will no doubt wish to visualize the way in which "your own self" corresponds to the general pattern. The importance of this approach is seen when the result is that you as an individual begin the engaging and worthwhile journey toward self-modification of behavior. This is always at some level a renewing and enlightening human experience.

The total personality encompasses all the above major aspects of personality. All of these components are highly interrelated and interdependent. All of the components are important to the balance and health of the personality—because only when these individual components function in a healthy way can the *personality as a whole* maintain a completely healthy state. The condition of any one component affects each other aspect to a degree, and hence the personality as a whole.

When a nervous person stutters or becomes nauseated, it is not necessarily a mental state that is causing the physical symptom. On the contrary, a pressure imposed upon the body causes a series of reactions, which includes thought, verbalization, digestive processes, and muscular function. Mind alone does not always cause the body to become upset. The *total* body is upset by a situation, and reflects its upset in several ways including disturbance in thought, feeling, and bodily processes. The whole individual responds in interaction with the social and physical environment. And, as the individual is affected by his or her environment, he or she in turn has an effect upon it. This is an especially important principle to understand regarding individuals who function in the emotionally charged, physically demanding athletics environment.

For decades, human development was studied and understood as physical development or intellectual development—a rigid and persistent dichotomy. However, more recent research demonstrates that the understanding of human development must be physical and intellectual development—properly designating the clear and compelling interrelationship of these human dimensions. Any authentic understanding of human development and human personality must embrace this fact. Otherwise we have a *dis*integrated view of the total person.

In contemporary society great emphasis is placed on social development and social adjustment. Faulty interpersonal relationships (causes, consequences, and remediation) are a major area of study and publication. For this reason it is important to understand the interaction between the individual and the environment. The quality of the individual's interpersonal relationships affect all other aspects of his or her personality. How well do you drive a car when someone is shouting at you? How well can you concentrate when you think someone is talking about you? How well will an athlete perform if a coach constantly berates him or her? These are social circumstances which affect the physical, emotional, and intellectual aspects of personality.

All of these dimensions are therefore the primary basis of total personality—a complex balance of psychological, physical, and social considerations that prepare the individual for the fullest, most socially valuable, productive, and adventuresome living. A large portion of the responsibility to develop a balanced and winsome life falls to the individual. This is only possible for any of us as we continuously make adjustments and modifications in personal behavior that will in one way or another add to our quality of living—and thereby assist us in prevention and management of undesirable stress.

SELF-CONCERNS THAT CAN INDUCE STRESS

Any discussion of the dimensions of *selfhood* needs to include the stress-inducing factors that involve personal or self concerns. The following descriptive sections address a few of these important personal concern factors.

Self-Concerns Associated with the Meeting of Personal Goals

Setting goals that are too demanding and too difficult to accomplish results in stress. For example, goals may be much higher than a particular environment will permit one to achieve. We often see coaches or athletic directors who set goals for their teams and programs for which there are no traditions or financial, personnel, or physical plant resources present to achieve those lofty goals. Likewise, we have seen teams set achievement goals (such as a winning season or postseason tournament or bowl participation) when in fact there is an absence of talent (or other existing condition) that makes achievement of the goal unlikely or impossible. The continuous failure to achieve goals of this kind can result in serious stress and morale issues. On the contrary, if one sets goals that are too low, he or she may develop a sense of underachievement or boredom even though the modest goals are achieved. These aspects of stress are also related to the *fear* that some persons have that they will not reach the goals to which they aspire—or the *fear* that their modest goals, even when achieved, will not be viewed by others as significant or worthy.

Self-Concerns That Involve Self-Esteem

This concern is related to the way one feels about oneself. Indeed, self-esteem is often related to the fulfillment of certain *ego needs*. It is troubling to some people that their superiors (coaches/ athletes) do not praise them for what they consider to be very adequate or outstanding performance. It is also quite stressful for some young athletes who feel that their perceived role on the team is not as valuable or appreciated as they deserve. This is a characteristic of many young adults, as well as older adults, regardless of their pursuits. Ego needs such as recognition are some of the most compelling human psychological needs—and often result in highly stressful conditions.

Self-Concerns Related to Changing Values

It is frustrating to many individuals if they feel that the value system in a given environment does not meet their own standards. They may develop the perception that some individuals are not inclined to place a value on those factors that they feel are important to their own growth and development. This threat to or lack of a general appreciation for an individual's core values can produce significant levels of stress. This is especially true when a disagreeing individual is in an athletics team environment where shared goals and values are often the driving dynamic underlying the entire team experience.

Self-Concerns That Center Around Social Needs

In some cases athletes may feel that their own social life is unfairly neglected because of the demands of time spent in athletics-related activities. This is a concern voiced by many athletes (and their friends and significant others).

Self-Concerns Involving Personal Competence and Ability

This is probably the self-concern that frustrates some athletes more than any other. Certainly, lack of confidence in one's ability can be devastating to morale and consequently result in diminishing effort or withdrawal.

It should be mentioned that not all of these self-concerns are characteristic of everyone, particularly because of the wide individual differences among them. That is, what may be a serious self-concern for one person may be a minimal concern for another. But they as a group do encompass perhaps a majority of those self-related concerns shared by the people who make up most populations, clearly including those persons involved in athletics programs.

PROCESSES OF BEHAVIORAL ADJUSTMENT

The term *adjustment* can be described as the process of finding and adopting modes of behavior suitable to the environment or to changes in the environment.

Life involves a continuous sequence of experiences that are strongly marked by the necessity for the human organism to adjust. Consequently, it may be said that "normal" behavior is the result of successful adjustment, and abnormal behavior results from unsuccessful adjustment. The degree of adjustment that the individual achieves depends upon how adequately he or she is able to satisfy basic needs and to fulfill desires within the framework of the environment—while employing behaviors that are generally acceptable within society.

As mentioned previously, stress may be considered as any factor acting internally or externally that renders adaptation difficult, and which induces increased effort on the part of the person to maintain a state of equilibrium within himself or herself and with the external environment. When stress is induced as a result of the person not being able to meet needs (basic demands) and to satisfy desires (wants or wishes), *frustration* or *conflict* results.

Frustration occurs when a need is not met and conflict results when choices must be made between almost equally attractive alternatives or when basic emotional forces oppose one another. In the emotionally healthy individual the degree of frustration is ordinarily in proportion to the intensity of the need or the desire. That is, one will objectively observe and evaluate the situation to ascertain whether a solution is possible—and if so, then what solution would best enable him or her to achieve the fulfillment of needs and desires. However, every person has a "zone of tolerance," or limits for physical, physiological, and psychological stress within which he or she normally operates. If the stress becomes considerably greater than the tolerance level, or if the individual has not learned to cope with his or her problems (and objectively and intelligently solve them), some degree of maladjustment can result.

SOME GENERAL PROCEDURES
FOR SELF-MODIFICATION OF BEHAVIOR

Over the years a great amount of literature has been published in the general area of behavior modification. This information has been directed to school administrators, teachers, counselors, and parents for the purpose of utilizing that procedure to produce behavior change in students. Here, we are concerned with self-modification of behavior for the purpose of preventing and managing stress.

Although self-modification of behavior may be considered by some to be a relatively recent innovation, it was used effectively in the early history of our country by Benjamin Franklin.[1] He is said to have used it to improve upon such virtues as patience, temperance, and frugality. He kept a record of the errors he thought he made each day related to over a dozen virtues. At the end of the day, he would consult the information to get feedback to help him identify those virtues that he may have violated or that he had missed an opportunity to manifest in his life. In modern times our approach to self-modification of behavior is more sophisticated than that of Franklin, with improvement in procedures constantly being made. Indeed, the body of information in the general area of self-modification of behavior has increased at a rapid pace over the past decade, while our understanding of human stress has also increased greatly.

Whether one is attempting to modify behavior of another (coach with an athlete) or trying to modify his or her own behavior, the general procedures of application are essentially the same. There are certain sequential steps to be taken that include the following: (a) identification and description of one's behavior, (b) counting behaviors, (c) attempting to effect a change in behaviors, and (d) evaluating the procedures used to change behaviors. The following sections will discuss some of the important features involved in these important steps.

Identifying Behaviors

The first step in the process is identifying a behavior that one wishes to modify. This process is also referred to as *targeting, isolating,* or *specifying* a behavior. Essentially this involves trying to define a particular behavior (target) that one wishes to change. This is not always an easy matter because a person may manifest a behavior that is annoying to others, but he or she may be completely unaware of it.[2]

When a person is able to identify a particular behavior and admit that such a behavior may be interfering with social relationships (vocational or interpersonal), a viable beginning can be made toward behavioral change. In other words, recognizing that one has a problem is the first prerequisite to solving it.

In many instances, the identification of a behavior emerges when one is dissatisfied with what he or she may be doing and/or the results of their behavior.[3] For example, a person may find that he or she may be performing a behavior he or she does not want to perform, or in another case that he or she may be performing a behavior he or she wants to perform. The practice of analyzing the level of satisfaction/dissatisfaction with a given behavior, especially when results of the behavior are considered, is a highly useful exercise.

In the following discussion a *hypothetical model* of self-modification of behavior is depicted. The basic principles of the model apply almost uniformly to the behaviors of a coach toward his or her student-athletes.

Kim, the captain of the women's varsity soccer team, is a college senior majoring in elementary education. She is also doing her student teaching in a sixth-grade classroom.

Kim is also enrolled in a late afternoon required course titled, "Psychology of Teaching." In one class session on the general topic of "teacher attention," the discussion focused upon inappropriate teacher response to a student's behavior. That is, when there is a noise the teacher commands, "Be quiet!" Or, when students are out of their seats, the teacher commands, "Sit down!" It was also revealed that the emphatic "sit down" commands actually increase the frequency of standing behavior among students.

Kim not only recognized that she had been performing this behavior in her student teaching, but also observed that on occasion it had degenerated into a shouting match with students, creating a highly stressful situation. Inwardly she had been dissatisfied with herself for performing this behavior, but had neglected to do anything about it. Upon learning that this form of behavior could make an undesirable situation even worse, she felt a desperate need to try to correct it. She had identified an inappropriate behavior and was ready for the next step in self-modification of behavior, that of *counting* behaviors.

Counting Behaviors

The second step in self-modification of behavior is concerned with actually counting how often a target behavior occurs (noting the frequency or pervasiveness of the behavior). This means that one obtains a frequency count of the behavior to be improved.[4] If this step is not taken, it is difficult to learn the extent to which the targeted behavior is being performed. Quite often, simply counting a behavior will tend to improve it because the person is becoming involved in self-awareness of the behavior. This is to say that counting a behavior calls one's attention to it and how often it is occurring.

In addition to determining the frequency of a behavior, another aspect of this counting step is what is called the *ABC Factor* in the behavior modification approach. That is, Antecedent of the behavior, the Behavior itself, and the Consequence of the behavior. Antecedent is concerned with any event that preceded the behavior and consequence is what happens as a result of the behavior. The following examples of the "ABCs of behavior" occurred in Kim's student teaching experience:

	Antecedent	Kim's Behavior	Consequence
Item 1	Student gets out of seat.	Kim shouts at student to "Sit down!"	Class laughs at Kim.
Item 2	Student talks out to another student.	Kim shouts at student to "Be quiet!"	Student gives Kim a bored look.
Item 3	Student falls asleep.	Kim claps hands close to student's ears and awakens him.	Disruption of class by laughter of other students.

Obviously, it is most important that a person develop an awareness of antecedents and consequences of behaviors. The primary reason for this is that an antecedent gets a behavior started and then that behavior can result in an unsatisfactory consequence, as in the above illustration. We have seen this sequence played out frequently in athletics settings, especially in the coach-team relationship.

Attempting to analyze an antecedent becomes important in regard to a manifested behavior. That is, *why did the antecedent occur in the first place?* This is a critically important question. In the case of the above classroom example, questions such as the following might be raised:

> Item 1. Why did the student leave his or her seat? Was he or she justified in doing so? Did Kim react too quickly?
>
> Item 2. Why did a student talk out to another student? Was this a persistent behavior of this particular student?
>
> Item 3. Why did the student fall asleep? Was he or she ill? Had he or she done this before, or was this the first time?

The information derived from step two will provide what is termed *baseline data.* If the information is valid and the behavior frequency is accurate, the person has a base from which to move forward. This means that one will be in a position (with sufficient information) to see if attempts at improving a given behavior (step three, changing behavior) is meeting with satisfactory results.

Changing Behaviors

The effort to change a behavior that has been identified, described, counted, and recorded is referred to as a *plan of intervention.* That is, the person intervenes with one or more procedures designed to modify the inappropriate behavior. Any plan to replace an inappropriate behavior with an appropriate one involves some kind of reinforcement procedure. Generally speaking, self-reinforcement is concerned with changing behavior through self-produced consequences, and these consequences may be overt or covert. Examples are: (a) statements being made to oneself, or (b) the acquisition of an item as a reward for one's efforts.

To help in the clarification of step three, let us return to the case of Kim. It will be recalled that she was dissatisfied with her constant criticism of, and shouting at, some of her sixth-grade students. She had gone through steps one and two by identifying a target behavior and gathering information about frequency of occurrence, along with an analysis of antecedents and consequences.

In her course in the "Psychology of Teaching" one of the topics for discussion was "teacher praise versus teacher criticism" in dealing with students. Recognizing that her behavior with her sixth-grade class was predominantly characterized by criticism, she took as her term project a study of these two factors—teacher praise and teacher criticism. Her investigation into the literature on the subject revealed the following information.

1. Teacher behavior in such forms as smiles and words of encouragement, if made contingent upon an appropriate student behavior, tend to increase the frequency of that behavior. Therefore, these forms of teacher behavior function as reinforcers for many student behaviors. (This suggested to Kim that she consider minimizing criticism of inappropriate student behavior and maximizing praise for appropriate behavior.)

2. Teacher behavior that ignores inappropriate student behavior can be effective in diminishing that behavior. This, of course, depends upon how disruptive and/or dangerous the behavior might be. Obviously, some types of student behavior cannot be ignored. (This suggested to Kim that the time she was using to criticize one student for inappropriate behavior might well be spent praising another for appropriate behavior.)

3. Teacher behavior in the form of criticism should not be neglected entirely, but rather there should be a propitious ratio between praise and criticism, with the former occurring about five times as often as the later. (It has been demonstrated that such a ratio can achieve success. Moreover, it has been shown that when things are going poorly in the classroom, teachers criticize students about four or five times more than they praise them. Kim's behavior had been almost entirely one of criticism.)

4. When a teacher criticizes a student, it can be done quietly. Conversely, when praise is given it can be done with emphasis. Thus, a general principle might be to maximize the tone of praise and

minimize the tone of criticism. The importance of this has been borne out in studies showing that a loud tone of criticism may likely cause more inappropriate behavior of some students while soft tones may contribute to better control situations. (Kim remembered that frequently she had resorted to shouting at students.)

5. It may be a good practice for a teacher to criticize an inappropriate behavior without heaping too much criticism on a student. For example, a teacher could emphasize the fact that a student is a "good person" but that the behavior was not so good. Or, from a negative orientation, "You are not a bad person, but what you did was not acceptable behavior."

With the above information to use as a guideline, Kim was ready to formulate a plan of intervention. The major objective was to make an effort to reduce or eliminate the inappropriate behavior of criticism accompanied by shouting and replace it with a more appropriate behavior.

Kim's task was to intervene with activities that would have some influence on the above situation and also to provide for self-reinforcement when such behaviors were performed. The following items were used in the intervention plan:

1. An effort was made to use less criticism, based upon the level of undesirability of a given student behavior.
2. An effort was made to use praise for appropriate behavior, not only of a verbal nature but also in the form of smiling, nods of approval, and the like.
3. A new voluntary seating plan was devised for the purpose of separating those students who tended to talk out to each other.
4. Cooperative assistance from some of the students was enlisted. This took the form of noting for Kim when she tended to perform an inappropriate behavior. This action on the part of Kim indicated to the students that she was "human" after all.

The next point of concern was that of self-reinforcement. It should be recalled that self-reinforcement is concerned with overt or covert consequences in the form of statements to oneself or the acquisition of an item as a reward for one's efforts. Kim decided that the major form of self-reinforcement would involve self-praise, or what is referred to as "stroking." There is a strong human need to be applauded for a successful effort, if not by someone else, then by oneself. Kim treated herself to dinner at a nice restaurant when significant progress had been observed.

In our hypothetical model, a plan was also introduced by Kim whereby when any member of the class did well in something, that person literally gave himself or herself a pat on the back. This also included Kim—and it became a common practice for her, as well as the class members, to applaud themselves for any worthy achievement. This became a compelling and positive dynamic within the culture of the classroom.

Evaluating the Plan of Intervention

The final step in self-modification of behavior is to assess how well the plan of intervention is succeeding, that is, the extent to which the changes in behavior are achieving desired results. This process requires development of valid evaluative criteria. These criteria can be broad in scope, and thus apply to any problem of self-modification of behavior, or they can be more specific and be applied to a particular case. Some examples of general criteria might include the following:

1. In general, was there an increase in appropriate behavior and/or a decrease in inappropriate behavior?
2. What were the behaviors that achieved the most satisfactory results?
3. What forms of reinforcement appeared to be most successful?

These general evaluative criteria could be applied more specifically in our hypothetical case as follows:

1. Did Kim notice fewer instances of criticism and shouting on her part by actually keeping an account of this type of behavior? If so, how many?
2. Did the voluntary change in seating plan have any influence on the students who had been obtrusively talking out? If so, in how many instances?

3. Did the system of "patting ourselves on the back" help as a reinforcer in behavior change? If so, in how many ways?

These are a few ways to evaluate the plan of intervention. But there is still another decision to be made—when to terminate. This decision is related to the extent to which the plan has achieved success. If the plan has met with complete and unequivocal success, it can then perhaps be terminated. Or, if it succeeds only when the behavior change is still being practiced, there may be a need to maintain the procedure. The ultimate goal should be to modify behavior to the extent that the stressful problem is eliminated. This can be accomplished if one systematically and carefully carries out the general procedures outlined above. Experience has shown that one can modify his or her own behavior not only to *correct* stress arousal but to *avoid* it as well. This is most certainly the case in the athletics environment.

SYSTEMATIC SELF-DESENSITIZATION

A form of behavior modification known as *systematic desensitization* can be described as *the process of systematically lessening a specific learned fear in an individual*. It is purported to provide one means of controlling anxiety. If one can accomplish this, it becomes an extremely important factor in reducing stress. The reason for this is that the individual becomes more able to control his or her fears and anxieties, rather than having them control him or her.

As a clinical psychotherapeutic procedure, systematic desensitization consists of presenting to the imagination of the deeply relaxed person the weakest item in a list of anxiety-evoking stimuli repeatedly, until no more anxiety is evoked. The next item of the list is presented, and so on, until eventually, even the strongest of the anxiety-evoking stimuli fails to evoke any stir of anxiety in the person.

It is the purpose of the remainder of this chapter to provide specific information about the process of self-desensitization and how this important technique can benefit the individual who can self-administer the technique effectively to reduce stress.

Originally, the focus of systematic desensitization was primarily upon counselor-client, therapist-patient, or teacher-student relationships (and could have appropriately included the coach-athlete relationship). It has been widely used as a behavior therapy technique.

Systematic desensitization has now gained favor as a self-administered technique. Although the value of it as a means of lessening stress-provoking situations has not been completely established by behavioral scientists, some of the research findings are quite encouraging. For example, studies have shown that systematic self-desensitization can be very effective in overcoming severe public speaking anxiety, test anxiety, and a host of other stress-invoking stimuli.

Clinical psychologists believe that systematic self-desensitization efforts are not likely to be harmful, even if they fail. However, self-desensitization should be approached as an experimental procedure and it should be discontinued if the course of anxiety-reduction is not relatively smooth and it should be discontinued immediately if any increase in anxiety is experienced.

Various behavioral therapists and clinical psychologists have set forth models for the practice of systematic self-desensitization. The following model seems to have universal applicability.

The subject of systematic desensitization is based upon the notion that many anxieties that people experience are due to what are termed *conditioned reactions*. These conditioned reactions are identified as stimuli that occur together in our experience and become associated with each other so that we respond to them in the same or similar way when they occur again. This is to say that if we are made anxious in the presence of certain stimuli these same stimuli will make us anxious later when they occur again, even if the situation in reality no longer poses an actual threat. An example is a person who may have had a number of experiences as a child in which a person in authority, such as a school principal, police officer, or guardian frightened the child and perhaps punished him or her in some way. As an adult, this person's reaction to someone in authority may produce more anxiety in them than the situation really justifies. This occurs because of his or her previous conditioning of strong anxiety to an authority figure.

Many of our emotions seem to be based on such conditioned reactions. And, these reactions are somewhat similar to reflexes, but they are learned rather than inherited (the reader may wish to refer to the earlier discussion of learned and unlearned tensions in Chapter 1). Their automatic "reflexive" nature, however, explains why it is difficult to discuss issues rationally with someone who is emotionally involved in a situation. He or she is responding more with his or her *conditioned* reactions to the present stimuli than relating to the actual realities of the situation.

Nevertheless, the helpful stress-management technique for overcoming anxieties that occur in the form of conditioned reactions is the use of systematic self-desensitization. A highly persuasive case can be made for its effectiveness, provided it is carried out properly.

After a particular stress-producing problem has been identified, the process consists of three sequential steps: (1) developing a hierarchy of anxiety-evoking stimuli, (2) complete relaxation, and (3) desensitization sessions. Using the previously mentioned authority figure example, let us make application of this to a college student who has profound relational difficulty with his advisor, the department chairperson. Incidentally, our surveys of college athletes show that it is not uncommon for some of them to experience what they designate as a "fear of the administrator" without being able to identify reasons for it.

Let us take the hypothetical case of Dave. Dave is a bone-crunching linebacker, but when it comes to coping with an authority figure, he seems to retreat into a shell.

Dave's first step is to acquire several index cards. He writes one situation or experience on each card that creates anxiety concerning his relationship with an authority figure. The cards are then arranged in order of the one causing the least anxiety on the top and the one causing the greatest anxiety at the bottom. This is the hierarchy of anxiety-evoking stimuli and might resemble the following:

1. Entering school parking lot and seeing department chairperson's car
2. Greeting fellow students and discussing department chairperson
3. Greeting fellow student who mentions his upcoming meeting with the department chairperson
4. Conferring with a fellow student after his meeting with the department chairperson

5. Walking by department chairperson's office when the door is closed
6. Walking by department chairperson's office when the door is open (no verbalization or eye contact)
7. Walking by department chairperson's office when the door is open (using eye contact and nodding)
8. Arranging meeting with the department chairperson through the secretary
9. Talking with department chairperson's secretary about the department chairperson
10. Prearranged meeting with department chairperson with only self present
11. Other meetings with department chairperson with only self present

The remaining self-desensitizing process is then carried out using the methods described in the following:

Another stress-inducing situation that concerns many individuals is that of presenting a report in front of a group. Coaches are sometimes required to make reports and speeches to boosters, alumni and other groups. This can be a stressful ordeal, especially if their team is losing. Some students have this same problem when presenting a report in front of a class. The following is a suggested hierarchy to use for self-desensitization for this purpose:

1. Reading an article about presenting reports
2. Reading the report alone
3. Reading report in front of a mirror
4. Reading report into tape recorder and playing it back
5. Reading report to a roommate
6. Reading report to roommate with one other present
7. Reading report with three others present
8. Reading report to two or three persons where there is a large gathering, such as in a dining hall or other public place
9. Entering the classroom
10. Member of audience while other reports are given
11. Giving report to entire class

Of course the reader must understand that the above hierarchies of anxiety-evolving stimuli are general in nature. Each individual would write his or her own list in more specific detail and pertaining more to specific anxieties.

The second step is to try to develop a condition of complete relaxation (the reader is referred to Chapter 7 for a review of the various relaxation procedures). It is recommended that the person go through each of the muscle groups in sequential order to learn to relax them one by one.

After the person is completely relaxed, the next step is to begin systematic self-desensitization. Look at the top card on the stack—the one that is the least anxiety-provoking. Ask the person to close his or her eyes, and using their imagination, visualize as vividly as possible the situation described on the card. That is, one imagines the situation occurring and that he or she is actually there. At this point, if some anxiety is experienced, the imaginary scene should cease immediately and the person should go back to relaxing. After complete relaxation is again achieved, the person is ready to proceed again. This procedure is continued until the scene can be imagined without anxiety. This may take only one or two times, or it could take ten to fifteen times, but it should be repeated until no anxiety is felt. The entire procedure is continued until one has gone through all the cards.

It is recommended that one work on the scenes in this manner for approximately one-half hour at a time. It can be done daily, every other day, or a couple times a week depending upon the amount of time one is willing or able to spend, and how quickly one wants to conquer the anxiety. It appears to be a good practice to overlap one or two items from one session to another; that is, beginning a session by repeating an item or two from the previous session that were imagined without anxiety.

One variation of the above procedure is to tape record a description of each scene in advance. One then relaxes and listens to the tape. If anxiety appears, the recorder is turned off and the person goes back to relaxing. When relaxation is again accomplished the individual proceeds as before. A value of using the tape recorder is that there is likely to be better pronunciation, enunciation, and intonation of words. In addition, it may be easier for the individual to concentrate, since he or she has provided his or her own auditory input on tape and does not have the additional task of verbalizing and trying to concentrate on the scene at the same time. If desired, the sequence of relaxation procedures can be taped for playback as well.

After one has achieved desensitization he or she can review in his or her own mind the preferred action to take in the situation that caused anxiety. Plans can be made to carry out a positive behavior the next time the situation occurs.

Obviously, the success one experiences with this procedure will depend largely upon the extent to which one is willing to make the considerable effort involved in the approach. Many persons who have tried it have been so delighted by its effects that they have deliberately sought out situations that previously had caused them great anxiety, frustration, and failure in order to deal with those situations.

While the effectiveness of various self-modification of behavior techniques will vary from person to person, the incontrovertible outcomes of these techniques appear overall to be very positive— for the general population and also for individuals involved as athletes and employees in the environment of college athletics.

Afterword

The pervasive presence of stress in our society is well-documented by social scientists, health professionals, and behavioral scientists. Its effects on the individual and on our culture have been the subject of a great deal of writing and public discussion.

The presence of stress-inducing conditions in the field of athletics has also drawn considerable attention and concern. In exploring the stress phenomenon in college athletics we have attempted to explain the meaning of stress in general as well as theories of stress. Its causes and effects and the coping techniques that are reportedly used to prevent or diminish stress were also examined.

In discussing the selected techniques that have had some success in stress reduction, we must point out that recommendations made throughout the book have met with varying degrees of success with persons who practiced them. Individual differences indicate that one person may find more success than another with given procedures. One of the most important factors to remember is that stress management is pretty much an individual matter. With practice, most persons will have some degree of success in their attempts to manage their own stressful conditions.

However, it is quite clear that a person under stressful conditions must have an *action plan* in order to deal effectively with stress. This personal stress-management system can include the useful information on stress discussed in this book and other sources (providing an understanding of stress) and can also include specific strategies discussed here and elsewhere which might prove to be enabling and empowering over stressful conditions. But the key is to have a personal plan for dealing with stress and implementing it systematically and faithfully. The desirable result will be that the individual begins to develop an *internal culture* of stress management. This internalized coping system will equip the individual to handle stressful conditions in a way that is balanced, reasonably comfortable, and usually, with fairly predictable outcomes. Simply stated, the individual will be able to *take control* of his or her stress.

The techniques for stress control that have been discussed in the foregoing chapters do not represent an exhaustive list of possible stress-management strategies. Indeed, there are many other proven methods. These other methods include, but are not limited to: counseling therapy; mentor influence and guidance; effective strategic planning for personal and professional decision making and action;[1] additional training in specific skills that are required to be used in an individual's work and relationships; and goal setting and goal management (a part of the strategic-planning process), along with numerous other formal and informal stress-reduction techniques.[2]

But what we have provided here is a discussion that focuses on the general phenomenon of stress and its manifestation in the athletics environment. This discussion, along with its exploration of a number of proven stress-management methodologies, will provide considerable food for thought in the athletics community and among other groups—and hopefully will serve as the basis for further research and inquiry.

Notes

Chapter 1

1. Rosch, Paul J. "Join Us in the Quest to Better Understand and Manage the Stress Syndrome," *Practical Stress Management: The Newsletter of the American Institute of Stress,* September 1983, p. 1.

2. Selye, Hans. *Stress Without Distress,* New York: New American Library, 1975, p. 17.

3. Humphrey, James H. *Job Stress,* Boston: Allyn and Bacon, 1998, p. 5.

4. Walker, C. Eugene. *Learn to Relax: 13 Ways to Reduce Tension,* Englewood Cliffs, NJ: Prentice-Hall, 1975, p. 16.

5. Viscott, David. *The Language of Feeling,* New York: Arbor House, 1976, p. 9.

6. *The New Columbia Encyclopedia,* Fourth Edition, s.v., "Depression," p. 748.

7. Malone, Christopher J. and Rotella, Robert J. "Preventing Coaching Burnout," *Journal of Health, Physical Education, Recreation and Dance,* November/December 1981, p. 37.

8. Thomas, William C. "Avoiding Burnout: Hardiness As a Stress Buffer in College Athletes," Reston, VA: *Research Quarterly for Exercise and Sports,* Supplement, 69, 1998, pp. 116-117.

9. Williams, Redford B. and Williams, Virginia. *Lifeskills,* New York: Random House, 1998, p. 63.

10. Cannon, Walter B. *The Wisdom of the Body,* New York: W.W. Norton and Co., Inc., 1932, p. 131.

11. Knox, George W. "Anti-Aging: A Triple Approach to Longevity," *Affirmative Awareness Newsletter,* Issue 1, 1997, p. 2.

12. Posner, Israel and Leitner, Lewis A. "Eustress vs. Distress: Determination by Predictability and Controllability of the Stressor," *STRESS, The Official Journal of the International Institute of Stress and Its Affiliates,* 2, Summer 1981, p. 5.

13. Porter, David T. and Allsen, Philip E. "Heart Rates of Basketball Coaches," *The Physician and Sports Medicine,* October 1978, p. 11.

Chapter 2

1. Gerdy, John R. *The Successful Athletic Program: A New Standard,* Phoenix, AZ: Ornyx Press/American Council on Education, 1997, p. 53.

2. Yow, Deborah A. "Quality Issues in Contemporary Intercollegiate Athletics," Printed lecture notes, 1996, p. 2.

3. Humphrey, James H. *Job Stress,* Boston: Allyn and Bacon, 1998, p. 11.

Chapter 3

1. Humphrey, James H. *Helping Children Manage Stress,* Washington, DC: Child and Family Press, 1998, p. 14.
2. Kearney, Helen McCready. "Female stress: An overview," *Practical Stress Management, The Newsletter of the American Institute of Stress,* May/June 1985, p. 17.
3. McQuade, Walter and Aikan, Ann. *Stress,* New York: E.P. Dutton and Company, Inc., 1974, p. 31.
4. Bowden, William W. "Stress Management in Contemporary Society," Guest lecture, St. Louis University, St. Louis, MO, 1998.
5. Frankenhaeuser, Marianne. "Women Are Said to Differ in Their Response to Stress," *Psychiatric News,* June 18, 1975, p. 20.
6. Humphrey, Joy N. and Everly, George S. "Perceived Dimensions of Stress Responsiveness in Male and Female Students," *Health Education,* November/December 1980, p. 38.
7. Rosch, Paul J. "More Headlines About Job Stress and Health," *The Newsletter of the American Institute of Stress,* No. 7, 1999, p. 1.
8. Rosch, Paul J. "Are Women More Stressed Out Than Men?", *The Newsletter of the American Institute of Stress,* No. 7, 1993, p. 6.
9. Bowden, William W. Interview with NCAA Division I student-athlete, Ohio, 1998.
10. Yow, Deborah A., Humphrey, James H., and Bowden, William W. "College Athletes Under Stress," *Athletics Administration,* December 1998, p. 17.
11. *Alcohol Alert.* Pamphlet published by the National Institute of Alcohol Abuse and Alcoholism, Bethesda, MD: April 1996, p. 2.

Chapter 4

1. *Webster's Ninth New Collegiate Dictionary.* Springfield, MA: Merriam-Webster, Inc., 1983.
2. "Fry Honored," *USA Today,* February 1999, p. 10C.
3. Walton, Gary M. *Beyond Winning,* Champaign, IL: Leisure Press, 1992, p. 112.
4. Copeland, B.W. and Kirsch, S. "Perceived Occupational Stress Among NCAA Division I, II, and III Athletic Directors," *Journal of Sport Management,* Champaign, IL: January 1995, p. 17.
5. Humphrey, James H. *Job Stress,* Needham Heights, MA: Allyn & Bacon, 1998, p. 33.
6. "Fight, Flight, or Flow?" *The Newsletter of the American Institute of Stress,* No. 5, 1992, p. 4.
7. Gerdy, John R. *The Successful Athletic Program: The New Standard,* Phoenix, AZ: Oryx Press/The American Council On Education, 1997, pp. 94-95.

Chapter 5

1. Gazes, P.C., Sovell, B.F., and Dellastatious, J.W. "Continuous Radioelectro-Cardiographic Monitoring of Football and Basketball Coaches During Games," *American Heart Journal*, October 1969, p. 34.

2. Husman, B.F., Hanson, D., and Walker, R. "The Effects of Coaching Basketball and Swimming Upon Emotions As Measured by Telemetry," In G.S. Kenyon (Ed.), *Contemporary Psychology of Sport*, International Association of Sports Psychology, 1970, p. 11.

3. Porter, David T. and Allsen, Philip E. "Heart Rates of Basketball Coaches," *The Physician and Sports Medicine*, October 1978, p. 21.

4. McCafferty, William B., Gliner, Jeffery A., and Horvath, Steven M. "The Stress of Coaching," *The Physician and Sports Medicine*, February 1978, p. 17.

5. Bowden, William W. Guest Lecture Notes: "Coaches As Teachers, Coaches As Leaders," Texas Tech University, Lubbock, TX, 1996.

6. Yow, Deborah A. Lecture Notes: "The Roles and Power of Emotion in Intercollegiate Athletics," University of Maryland, College Park, MD, 1997.

Chapter 6

1. "Stress and Cholesterol." *The Newsletter of the American Institute of Stress*, Yonkers, NY, No. 3, 1993, p. 6.

2. Rosch, Paul J. "Are There Stress Reducing Foods and Diets?", *The Newsletter of the American Institute of Stress*, Yonkers, NY: No. 10, 1994, p. 5.

3. *Nutrition Action Health Letter*, September 1997, p. 2.

4. *Diagnostic and Statistical Manual of Mental Disorders*, Fourth Edition. Washington, DC: American Psychiatric Association, 1994, pp. 544-545.

5. Ibid., pp. 549-550.

6. Anthony, William A. *The Art of Napping*, New York: Larson Publications, 1997, p. 7.

7. *Exercise and Your Heart* may be obtained free of charge by writing to the Consumer Information Center, Department P, Pueblo, CO 81009.

Chapter 7

1. Brown, Barbara B. *Stress and the Art of Biofeedback*, New York: Bantam Books, Inc., 1988, p. 44.

2. Benson, Herbert. *The Relaxation Response*, New York: William Morrow and Company, Inc., 1975, p. 36.

3. Rosch, Paul J. "Stress and Muscle Tension," *Health and Stress, The Newsletter of the American Institute of Stress*, No. 7, 1997, p. 2.

4. For detailed information on this program see Stroebel, Charles F. *The Quieting Reflex: A Six-Second Technique for Coping With Stress, Anytime, Anywhere*, New York: G.P. Putnam's Sons, 1982.

Chapter 8

1. Pelletier, Kenneth R. *Mind As Healer, Mind As Slayer,* New York: Dell, 1977, p. 6.

2. Woolfolk, Robert L. and Richardson, Frank C. *Stress, Survival & Society,* New York: New American Library, Inc., 1978, p. 68.

3. Benson, Herbert. *The Relaxation Response,* New York: William Morrow and Company, Inc., 1975, p. 41.

4. Hales, Diane and Hales, Robert. "Exercising The Psyche," *Health Weekly Journal of Medicine, Fitness, and Psychology,* June 5, 1985, p. 3.

5. Sethi, Amarjit S. *Meditation As an Intervention in Stress Reactivity.* In *Stress in Modern Society,* James H. Humphrey (Ed.), New York: AMS Press, No. 12, 1989, p. 16.

6. Goleman, Daniel J. and Schwartz, G.E. "Meditation As an Intervention in Stress Reactivity," *Journal of Consulting and Clinical Psychology,* 44, 1976, p. 32.

7. Wallace, R.K. "Physiological Effects of Meditation," *Science,* 167, 1970, p. 42.

8. Klemons, Ira M. "Change in Inflammation in Persons Practicing Transcendental Meditation Techniques." In *Scientific Research on Transcendental Meditation Program, Collected Papers,* 1, David W. Orme-Johnson and John T. Farrow (Eds.), New York: MIU Press, 1975, p. 9.

9. Shaw, Robert and Kolb, David. "One Point Reaction Time Involving Meditators and Nonmeditators." In *Scientific Research of Transcendental Meditation Program, Collected Papers,* 1, David W. Orme-Johnson and John T. Farrow (Eds.), New York: MIU Press, 1975, p. 13.

10. Kirsch, I. and Henry, D. "Self-Sensitization and Meditation in the Reduction of Public Speaking Anxiety," *Journal of Consulting and Clinical Psychology,* 47, 1979, p. 17.

11. Hall, N.R. and Goldstein, A.L. "Think Well: The Chemical Links Between Emotions and Health," *The Sciences,* March/April, 1986, p. 11.

12. Miskiman, Donald E. "The Effect of Transcendental Meditation Technique On The Organization of Thinking and Recall." In *Scientific Research on the Transcendental Meditation Program, Collected Papers,* 1, David W. Orme-Johnson and John T. Farrow (Eds.), New York: MIU Press, 1975, p. 23.

13. Tojoa, Andre S. "Some Evidence That the Transcendental Meditation Program Increases Intelligence As Measured by Psychological Tests." In *Scientific Research on the Transcendental Meditation Program, Collected Papers,* David W. Orme-Johnson and John T. Farrow (Eds.), New York: MIU Press, 1975, p. 16.

14. Morse, Donald R. et al. "Examination Induced Stress in Meditators and Nonmeditators As Measured by Salivary Protein Changes," *Stress, The Official Journal of the International Institute of Stress and its Affiliates,* Autumn 1981, p. 14.

Chapter 9

1. Corson, John A. "Stress, Self-Concept, and Violence." In *Stress in Modern Society,* James H. Humphrey (Ed.), New York: AMS Press, Inc., No. 11, 1988, p. 7.

2. Brown, Barbara B. *New Mind New Body,* New York: Bantam Books, 1975; and *Stress and the Art of Biofeedback,* New York: Bantam Books, Inc., 1988.

3. Bowden, William W. Lecture, "Biofeedback As an Effective Stress Management Tool," University of Florida, Gainesville, FL, 1993.

Chapter 10

1. Knapp, T.J. and Shodahl, S.A. "Ben Franklin As a Behavior Modifier," *Behavior Therapy,* 5, 1974, p. 11.

2. Tolson, Dr. B.J. Interview by Bowden, William W., Houston, TX: 1997.

3. Martin, Garry and Pear, Joseph. *Behavior Modification,* Englewood Cliffs, NJ: Prentice-Hall, Inc., 1983, p. 22.

4. Miltenberger, Raymond G. *Behavior Modification,* Albany/Boston: Brooks/Cole Publishing Co., 1997, p. 18.

Afterword

1. Migliore, R.H., Yow, Deborah A., Bowden, William W., Stevens, Robert E., Louden, David L. *Strategic Planning in College Athletics*, Binghamton, NY: The Haworth Press, 2000, p. 15. Also, Yow, Deborah A. "Advice to Incoming Freshmen [Athletes]." In *Quantum Leap to Collegiate Athletics: A Guidebook for High School Athletes, Parents and Coaches,* Kei Gilbert (Ed.), Silver Spring, MD: Soros, Inc., 1995, p. 249.

2. Gilbert, Kei. *Quantum Leap to Collegiate Athletics: A Guidebook For High School Athletes, Parents and Coaches,* Silver Spring, MD: 1995, p. 206. Also, Minirth, Frank. *Worry-Free Living*, Nashville, TN: Thomas Nelson Publishers, 1989, selected chapters.

Suggestions for Further Reading

Aieinena, S. "Respect: The Missing Component of Modern Athletic Competition," *The Physical Educator,* 54, Fall 1997.

Brown, C. and Bohac, J. "Beyond Athletic Participation: Career Development Intervention with Student Athletes," *Journal of College Student Development,* 38, November/December 1997.

Frauenknecht, M. and Brylinsky, R. "The Relationship Between Problem-Solving and High-Risk Health Behaviors Among College Athletes," *Journal of Health Education,* 27, July/August 1996.

Gould, D. "Personal Motivation Gone Awry: Burnout in College Athletics," *Quest,* 48, August 1996.

James, B. and Collins, D. "Self-Presentational Sources of Competitive Stress During Performance," *Journal of Sport & Exercise Psychology,* 19, March 1996.

McCormack, A.S. "Drinking in Stressful Situations: College Men Under Pressure," *College Student Journal,* 30, March 1996.

Meade, J. "Burnout," *Teacher Magazine,* 9, Spring 1996.

"Men's and Women's Athletics at 306 NCAA Division I Institutions," *The Chronicle of Higher Education,* 44, April 3, 1998.

Naughton, J. "Why Athletes Are Vulnerable to Gambling," *The Chronicle of Higher Education,* 44, April 17, 1998.

Naughton, J. and Selingo, J. "A Point-Saving Scandal Rattles a University," *The Chronicle of Higher Education,* 44, April 10, 1998.

Noel, N.E. and Cohen, D.J. "Changes in Substance Use During Times of Stress: College Students the Week Before Exams," *Journal of Drug Education,* 27, April 1997.

Perrin, K.M. "Laugh at Stress! Creative Methods for Treating Stress Management," *Journal of Health Education,* 26, September/October 1995.

Petrie, T.A. and Stoever, S. "Academic and Nonacademic Predictors of Female Student Athletes' Academic Performance," *Journal of College Student Development,* November/December 1997.

Raedek, T.G. "Is Athlete Burnout More Than Just Stress? A Sports Commitment Perspective," *Journal of Sport & Exercise Psychology,* 19, December 1997.

Schilling, T. "Stress Busters For Coaches," *Strategies,* 12, November/December 1998.

Schroeder, K. "Life After Athletics," *Education Digest,* 62, January 1997.

Selingo, J. "In College Sports Is Bigger Better?", *The Chronicle of Higher Education,* 44, October 31, 1997.

Scott, D.K. "Managing Organizational Culture in Intercollegiate Athletic Organizations," *Quest,* 49, November 1997.

Shuford, B.N. and Butler, D.W. "Keeping the Student Athlete on Track," *Coach and Athletic Director,* 67, March 1998.

Tricker, R. and Connolly, D. "Drugs and the College Athlete: An Analysis of the Student Athlete at Risk," *Journal of Drug Education,* 27, February 1997.

Vann, A.S. "From Burned Out to Fired Up!," *The Education Digest,* 61, November 1995.

Wrisberg, C.A. "Quality of Life for Male and Female Athletes," *Quest,* 48, August 1996.

Index

Order Your Own Copy of
This Important Book for Your Personal Library!

STRESS IN COLLEGE ATHLETICS
Causes, Consequences, Coping

_____ in hardbound at $59.95 (ISBN: 0-7890-0934-X)

_____ in softbound at $24.95 (ISBN: 0-7890-0935-8)

COST OF BOOKS _____

OUTSIDE USA/CANADA/
MEXICO: ADD 20% _____

POSTAGE & HANDLING _____
(US: $3.00 for first book & $1.25
for each additional book)
Outside US: $4.75 for first book
& $1.75 for each additional book)

SUBTOTAL _____

IN CANADA: ADD 7% GST _____

STATE TAX _____
(NY, OH & MN residents, please
add appropriate local sales tax)

FINAL TOTAL _____
(If paying in Canadian funds,
convert using the current
exchange rate. UNESCO
coupons welcome.)

☐ **BILL ME LATER:** ($5 service charge will be added)
(Bill-me option is good on US/Canada/Mexico orders only;
not good to jobbers, wholesalers, or subscription agencies.)

☐ Check here if billing address is different from
shipping address and attach purchase order and
billing address information.

Signature _____

☐ **PAYMENT ENCLOSED: $** _____

☐ **PLEASE CHARGE TO MY CREDIT CARD.**

☐ Visa   ☐ MasterCard   ☐ AmEx   ☐ Discover
☐ Diner's Club

Account # _____

Exp. Date _____

Signature _____

Prices in US dollars and subject to change without notice.

NAME _____

INSTITUTION _____

ADDRESS _____

CITY _____

STATE/ZIP _____

COUNTRY _____ COUNTY (NY residents only) _____

TEL _____ FAX _____

E-MAIL_____
May we use your e-mail address for confirmations and other types of information? ☐ Yes   ☐ No

Order From Your Local Bookstore or Directly From
The Haworth Press, Inc.
10 Alice Street, Binghamton, New York 13904-1580 • USA
TELEPHONE: 1-800-HAWORTH (1-800-429-6784) / Outside US/Canada: (607) 722-5857
FAX: 1-800-895-0582 / Outside US/Canada: (607) 772-6362
E-mail: getinfo@haworthpressinc.com
PLEASE PHOTOCOPY THIS FORM FOR YOUR PERSONAL USE.

BOF96

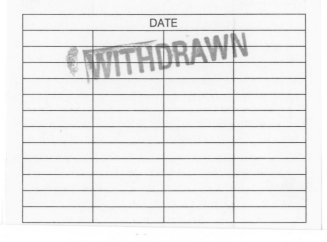